Peace

Jesus' Way of Shalom

Stephen D. Jones

Author of *Rabbi Jesus, Learning from the Master Teacher*

Peaceteacher
Jesus' Way of Shalom

Stephen D. Jones

Trafford Publishing
Victoria, British Columbia
on behalf of the
Baptist Peace Fellowship of North America
Charlotte, NC

Contents

Biblical quotations, unless otherwise noted, are from the New Revised Standard Version of the Bible (NRSV).

Peaceteacher
Jesus' Way of Shalom

Note for Librarians: A cataloguing record for this book is available from Library and Archives Canada at www.collectionscanada.ca/amicus/index-e.html
ISBN 1-4251-1943-3

Printed in Victoria, BC, Canada. Printed on paper with minimum 30% recycled fibre.
Trafford's print shop runs on "green energy" from solar, wind and other environmentally-friendly power sources.

Offices in Canada, USA, Ireland and UK

Book sales for North America and international:
Trafford Publishing, 6E–2333 Government St.,
Victoria, BC V8T 4P4 CANADA
phone 250 383 6864 (toll-free 1 888 232 4444)
fax 250 383 6804; email to orders@trafford.com
Book sales in Europe:
Trafford Publishing (UK) Limited, 9 Park End Street, 2nd Floor
Oxford, UK OX1 1HH UNITED KINGDOM
phone +44 (0)1865 722 113 (local rate 0845 230 9601)
facsimile +44 (0)1865 722 868; info.uk@trafford.com
Order online at:
trafford.com/07-0350

10 9 8 7 6 5 4 3 2

The woodcut, "Jesus the Teacher," on the front cover
is by the artist Solomon Raj, of India.
Used by permission.

Dedicated in Memory of Emma Lou Benignus,
my peaceteacher and friend

"The Shalom of God is as if someone would scatter seed on the ground, and would sleep and rise night and day, and the seed would sprout and grow, he does not know how. The earth produces of itself, first the stalk, then the head, then the full grain in the head."
(Mark 4:26-28)

The Shalom of God is near, even before we recognize it. It is always coming, not yet in full growth, but an emerging sprout of new growth.

Introduction

Jesus was a peaceteacher. His teachings reflect his vision of peace:

> peace with God,
> peace with the world,
> peace with oneself,
> peace among Jesus' followers,
> peace with one's enemies and
> peace with creation.

When Jesus spoke of peace, he used the Hebrew word, shalom. To the Jews, shalom is holistic. It isn't only about nonviolence or cessation of hostilities. Indeed, there could hardly be a more positive word. "Shalom is an iridescent word, with many levels of meaning in Hebrew Scripture. The base denominator of its many meanings is well-being, wholeness, completeness."[1] To translate it as "peace" fails to capture its fuller meaning in Hebrew. Shalom certainly includes an absence of war and commitment to nonviolence, but it also has to do with personal wholeness and societal harmony. It has to do with seeking the well being and personal fulfillment of everyone. Shalom embraces justice and peace with oneself, with others, and with God. Its cognate, shalem, means wholeness of life and personal health. Shalom is a word of hope, describing the emerging Peace of God. Shalom has to do with living God's way with others, with society, and with the created order.

English lacks a word as rich in symbolism and meaning as this Hebrew word, but similar words are found in other languages. The Hawaiian word, aloha, has a similar meaning. Like shalom, aloha is a word of greeting, but it also expresses feelings of love, affection, gratitude, kindness, pity, compassion and grief. One author has said, "It has been said that the word 'aloha' actually has two definitions. 'Alo' means the center or heart of the universe, while 'ha' is the breath or spirit of the Creator...aloha makes our lives whole, gives power to our words, fills our actions with purpose and assures that our every thought is of benefit to each other and to the world around us."[2] In southern Africa, a Bantu word, ubuntu, can be translated as "I am because we are," or "a person becomes human through other persons." It implies a universal bond of sharing that connects humanity. It speaks of how we are connected to a universal or communal whole. It is one of the founding principles of the new republic of South Africa and was a rallying call against apartheid. Gandhi centered his nonviolent philosophy on the Sanskrit word, satyagraha, an underlying truth-force against which the powers of violence were powerless. Satyagraha was of profound significance to Martin Luther

King, Jr. as he formed his own convictions about nonviolent resistance. It is a word that implies struggle and gentleness, the political and spiritual. Satyagraha, shalom, aloha, and ubuntu are provocative words that call people to aspire to nonviolence, wholeness, unity and fulfillment. It requires a paragraph of English words to express the meaning of any of these single words.

The Gospel of Luke brackets Jesus' earthly life with the message of shalom. At the birth of Jesus, the angels sang, "Glory to God in the highest, and on earth shalom among those whom he favors!" (2:14) Toward the end of his life on Palm Sunday, the "whole multitude of his disciples began to praise God joyfully with a loud voice" singing a message of shalom. (19:38) Then, weeping over the holy city, Jesus said, "If you had only recognized on this day the things that make for shalom!" (19:42) Luke presents shalom as the bookends holding Jesus' earthly life together.

Jesus was a peaceteacher who lived and taught shalom. There is no English word that better describes the essence of who Jesus was and what he taught. Scholars Hartmut Beck and Colin Brown state, "…the word (shalom) can describe both the content and goal of all Christian preaching, the message itself called 'the gospel of peace' (Eph 6:15; cf. Acts 10:36; Eph 2:17)."[3] Jesus invited his followers to come together as "children of shalom" (Lk 10:6) and he was "the only 1st-century Jew to whom this phrase is attributed…(It is) most likely a genuine coinage of Jesus." [4]

The Gospel of John is well-known for the "I am…" statements ascribed to Jesus. The author used these statements to express the uniqueness of Jesus, the way his identity forms and shapes our own identities. When he recorded Jesus as saying, "I am the light of the world," (8:12, 9:5) "I am the bread of life," (6:35, 48) "I am the living bread," (6:51) "I am the gate," (10:9) "I am the good shepherd," (10:11,14) "I am the resurrection and the life," (11:25) "I am the way, the truth and the life," (14:6) and "I am the true vine," (15:1) he employed the richest language possible to convey the meaning of Jesus' life. Though not repeated in the synoptic gospels, John's metaphors have held great meaning to Christians down through the centuries.

Another metaphor, "I am the pathway to shalom," could likewise faithfully communicate the message of Jesus. John wrote of Jesus as a messenger of shalom when Jesus began taking leave of the disciples on his final journey to Jerusalem. Once Jesus "knew that his hour had come to depart from this world" (13:1b), he said, "Shalom I leave with you, my shalom I give to you." (14:27) The Revised English Bible states, "Peace (shalom) is my parting gift to you, my own shalom…" Further conveying this conviction, he said, "I have said this to you, so that in me you may have shalom…" (16:33) Through Jesus' shalom, we find the pathway to our own shalom. In his resurrection appearances to the disciples, John recorded that Jesus greeted them twice saying, "Shalom be with you." (20:19c, 21a) "A week later,…Jesus came and stood among them and said, 'Shalom be with you.'" (20:26) According to John, Jesus not only taught about shalom, but in his death and resurrection, he became our pathway to shalom. As Paul wrote, "Christ is our peace." (Eph 2:14a) Jesus, our peaceteacher, "came and proclaimed peace to you who were far off and peace to those who were near..." (Eph 2:17) Jesus is the shalom of the world. The Peaceteacher offers the way of shalom, a way of holistic health, fulfillment, nonviolence, justice and well-being.

Shalom is a macro-concept. It is personal and public. It is spiritual and political. It is harmony and challenge. It is fulfillment of self and neighbor. It is familial and environmental. It is a way and a goal. It is here and not-yet. It involves becoming human and humane. It is not sectarian or exclusive. It doesn't embrace selfishness or greed. It is the opposite of violence and complacency.

If one embraces shalom, one embraces a philosophy toward life, an approach to living, a family of values leading to harmony and well-being. It doesn't result in cookie-cutter uniformity, but rather a broad spectrum of paths leading to shalom. Shalom is a holistic idea of external peace in the world and internal peace within. Peace without reconciliation typically leads to more violence. Shalom speaks to an authentic and full peace. Shalom is, simply put, the way God wants us to live together. Jesus offers shalom as God's Loving Intentionality for human beings.

It is awesome to state Jesus' teaching in a word: *shalom!* The wise teachings of any sage are often simple, though they represent deep mystery and profound truth. Simply by saying, shalom, doesn't mean we have captured the full meaning of Jesus' teachings. However, it does provide a shorthand way of describing his vision and wisdom. If something is un-shalom-like, then it isn't "of Jesus." It is that simple.

Shalom is not peripheral to Jesus' message, but at its core. Henri Nouwen wrote, "Peacemaking belongs to the heart of our Christian vocation; peacemaking is a full-time task for all Christians; and peacemaking has become in our century the most urgent of all Christian tasks."[5] Marcus Borg argues that the Jesus movement in the first century "was the peace party within Palestine" as it was a community "organized around compassion," the call to "love one's enemies," and a rejection of violent resistance to Rome.[6]

Jesus taught about the kingdom of God. About this nearly all scholars agree. The kingdom of (Heaven) God is mentioned fifty-four times in the Gospel of Matthew and thirty-nine times in the Gospel of Luke. "...most scholars hold that the proclamation of the reign (kingdom) of God was central to Jesus' teaching and actions...Jesus' proclamation of the kingdom of God permeates the Synoptic Gospels."[7] The kingdom of God "...stands at the very center of the message of the historical Jesus."[8] In the Gospel of Mark, Jesus launched his ministry by saying, "...the kingdom of God has come near..." (1:14b) By the kingdom of God, Jesus meant both a present and future reality, a realized and anticipated reign of God.

It is likely that Jesus first gave this phrase widespread usage. While the idea of God as King is found throughout Hebrew scripture, the phrase, kingdom of God, is not often found in Jewish or early rabbinical literature or indeed in other first century non-Christian writings. "...it has been a puzzle for New Testament scholars to determine where Jesus got the metaphor and why it is so central to his mission."[9] Jesus applied the kingdom of God in his first century world with bold vigor.

Even though central to Jesus' teachings, there is a serious hermeneutical problem as we speak of the kingdom of God today. It presents a challenge to our contemporary ear. We still have a few kings and queens in largely ceremonial roles in the world today, but they are mostly vestiges of former kingdoms. Kingdoms are an antiquated way of speaking of power or governance. It would be hard to imagine when the last new political kingdom was formed. When Jesus spoke about the kingdom of God, it was in a dynamic era when kingdoms were in vogue and the Roman Empire was at its zenith. Today, the concept of a kingdom raises troubling issues.

At a time when many around the world are concerned that U.S. America is acting more and more like an empire, one might easily confuse the kingdom of God with America as "a Christian nation." Those who want to impose their narrow interpretation of Christian morality upon the rest of the nation equate a partisan, right-wing agenda with the kingdom of God on earth.

The kingdom of God implies God's absolute rule over the world. A reigning God sounds imperialistic, all-powerful and triumphal. It suggests a God who towers over us, sitting on a throne of judgment. A ruling God controls our destiny, establishes the rules by which we must live and punishes law-breakers. God as King has the power and might to enforce the rules of his kingdom. Such a God is to be feared. It may be better to stay out of this monarch's way than risk his wrath.

In this light, the kingdom of God seems not to suggest a God of grace. Of course, these ideas are not what Jesus meant by the kingdom of God. The kingdom of which he spoke was one of reconciliation, grace and forgiveness. The difficulty for us comes in trying to communicate the Gospel using the metaphor of the kingdom of God. The kingdom of God, so anticipated among Jesus' first followers, does not describe the way many 21st century followers yearn for God.

Many thoughtful Christians today are trying to find another way of expressing Jesus' central message, acknowledging that "the kingdom of God" is fraught with implied meanings ill-suited for the twenty-first century. Rather than thinking of God as King, a "separate Being" who rules over us, many today consider God as Being itself, the source of life within us and throughout all creation. Marcus Borg offers a new perspective on God: "Rather than imagining God as a personlike being 'out there,' (a new) concept imagines God as the encompassing Spirit in whom everything that is, is. The universe is not separate from God, but in God…We are in God; we live in God, move in God, have our being in God. God is not 'out there,' but 'right here,' all around us."[10]

Other thoughtful Christians want to use less gender specific terms. But, masculine or feminine, regal language sets God over us rather than within us, around us, throughout all existence. A regal God is in conflict with a God who companions us, who stands beside us in this Present Moment, and who calls and empowers us to act with compassion, forgiveness and healing.

In my own spiritual journey, a regal God is less appealing. I don't experience God imposing his rule over my life or world. There is too much evil for that to be believable. Each person of faith must somehow locate God in his or her experience, and I don't experience God "over" me as much as under me, within me and beside me. Jesus said the kingdom of God is "at hand," (Mk 1:15; Lk 10:11b) meaning that we find God beside us. He said the kingdom of God is "among you," (Lk 17:21b) meaning we locate God between us. He said the kingdom of God is "within you," (Lk 17:21b NIV) meaning that we locate God within us. A regal, imperialistic God was the furthest thing from Jesus' idea of the kingdom of God.

It is little wonder that the central teaching of Jesus, the coming kingdom of God, is less frequently preached by the church today. As a preacher myself, I find it hard to use this phrase without going to great lengths to reinterpret it. Perhaps we need a better way to state what Jesus had in mind. Jesus himself seemed to struggle with how to speak of the kingdom of God. He once asked, "With what can we compare the kingdom of God, or what parable will we use for it?" (Mk 4:30)

Christianity has always been a translatable faith. The Apostle Paul felt called to translate the teachings and categories of the earthly Jesus into the Crucified and Risen Lord. Paul's language is startlingly different than that of Jesus as recorded in the four Gospels. It is a challenge to explain the difference between the language and thinking of the Gospels and that of the letters of the early church found in the Christian scripture. Willard Swartley believes that when Paul spoke of the "righteousness of God" he was conveying "a similar notion to the kingdom of God."[11] Even Jesus himself, by coining or popularizing the phrase, kingdom of God, was attempting to translate the historic Jewish faith so that those of his day could boldly hear it.

Christianity is a translated faith and we need to translate the kingdom of God so that twenty-first century people can better understand what Jesus had in mind in the first century. The issue isn't to improve Jesus' message, but rather for us to be able to hear what Jesus originally intended. The forward-leaning term Jesus used, both provocative and evocative in his day, sounds archaic in ours and beckons us backward.

Today, people might better respond to the Shalom of God, an anticipated time in which God's way of fulfillment, hope, well being, nonviolence and justice will be revealed. The Shalom of God expresses what Jesus meant as he spoke of the kingdom of God. The Shalom of God is "at hand" when all things work together as God intended. Jesus is the peaceteacher of the Shalom of God.

The Shalom of God is liberating to our 21st century concerns and offers a clarion call to our age. We can hear that call in these verses in which the kingdom of God (or Heaven) has been translated as the Shalom of God:

"The time is fulfilled, and the Shalom of God has come near; repent, and believe the Good News." Mk 1:15

"To you, my disciples, has been given the mystery of the Shalom of God, but for those outside, everything comes in parables..." Mk 4:11

"With what can I compare the Shalom of God?...It is like a mustard seed, which, when sown upon the ground, is the smallest of all the seeds on earth; yet when it is sown it grows up and becomes the greatest of all shrubs, and puts forth large branches, so that the birds of the air can make nests in its shade." Mk 4:30-33

"Not everyone who says to me, 'Lord, Lord' will receive the Shalom of God, but only the one who does the will of my Father in heaven." Mt 7:21

"Then Jesus went about all the cities and villages, teaching in their synagogues, and proclaiming the good news of shalom, and curing every disease and every sickness." Mt 9:35

"The Shalom of God is like a treasure hidden in a field, which someone found and hid; then in his joy he goes and sells all that he has and buys that field." Mt 13:44

"Therefore every scribe who has been trained for the Shalom of God is like the master of a household who brings out of his treasure what is new and what is old." Mt 13:52

"Truly I tell you, unless you change and become like children, you will never receive the Shalom of God." Mt 18:3
"Jesus said, 'Let the little children come to me, and do not stop them; for they are the children of shalom." Mt 19:14

"Truly I tell you, it will be hard for a rich person to receive the Shalom of God." Mt 19:23

This is what Jesus taught about the kingdom of God:

When the crowds found out about Jesus, they followed him; and he welcomed them, and spoke to them about the kingdom of God. (Lk 9:11) Jesus prayed, "Your kingdom come, O God, on earth as in heaven." (Mt 6:10) He taught: "The kingdom of God has come near. (Mk 1:15b) Indeed, it is already among you. (Lk 17:21) Here is my Good News: Receive the kingdom of God like a little child, (Lk 18:17) or as one who is born anew. (Jn 3:3) Strive for the kingdom of God." (Lk 12:31)

Now listen for the Shalom of God:

When the crowds found out about Jesus, they followed him; and he welcomed them, and spoke to them about the Shalom of God. Jesus prayed, "O God, may your shalom come on earth as in heaven." He taught: "The Shalom of God has come near. Indeed, it is already among you. Here is my Good News: Receive the Shalom of God like a little child, or as one who is born anew. Strive for the Shalom of God."

Jesus lived and taught shalom. The crux of his teaching can be communicated with two words: "Receive shalom." (Lk 18:17) We receive shalom through **spiritual centering** as we become receptive to the Spirit within. "The Shalom of God is within you." (Lk 17:21, TEV, NIV) We aren't asked to take control of shalom. We are asked to participate in shalom by making room for it in the center of our being. This is the Good News of Jesus' teaching (Mk 1:14-15), the definition of grace: **receive shalom.** We are to allow shalom a home within our lives. We are to let the Shalom of God eventually touch the core of our being, introducing wholeness and healing. We are to follow shalom as it touches others.

While we can't earn shalom, we can prepare for it. We needn't find God's shalom; it finds us. Jesus taught, "The Shalom of God is as if someone would scatter seed on the ground, and would sleep and rise night and day, and the seed would sprout and grow, he does not know how. The earth produces of itself, first the stalk, then the head, then the full grain in the head." (Mk 4:26-28) We know not how, but God introduces and nurtures shalom within us and throughout the whole of creation.

When shalom has been received, Jesus calls his followers to seek shalom (Mt 6:33a) above everything else. To seek shalom in all its breadth and depth is the **intentional centering** that complements spiritual centering. If we seek shalom first, then all personal needs and desires will take their rightful place. "...strive first for the kingdom of God,... and all these things will be given to you as well." (Mt 6:33). "Blessed are the peacemakers," Jesus said of intentional centering upon shalom. (Mt 5:9) If we are intentional about shalom, then we invest our prayerful energy into the fruits of shalom: harmony, nonviolence, justice, reconciliation and global healing.

Jesus talked of the kingdom of God for political reasons, primarily to challenge the reign of Caesar, the "divine ruler" of the known world. The Roman Peace (Pax Romana) was in actuality a peace secured by military might. In the kingdom of God, Jesus taught a different kind of peace. His provocative choice of terms clearly indicated a political challenge to the established kingdoms of his world. There would be no other reason to use such a loaded political term. Kingdom was the most political word of his day. When we speak of the Shalom of God, we are not referring only to inner peace. God's shalom, as with God's kingdom, involves personal and political peace. Shalom "has a public significance far beyond the purely personal."[12] To seek it first is to be engaged with and committed to the Shalom of God wherever we discern it.

Receive Shalom and Seek Shalom. Spiritual and Intentional Centering. It is both effortless and effortful. It involves receiving and becoming. This is the way Jesus offers. This is the truth Jesus offers. This is the life Jesus offers.

The more I study Jesus as a first century rabbi the more convinced I have become that his central message had to do with the Shalom of God. As his life unfolded, Jesus experienced different callings in his role as peaceteacher, callings important to consider as his disciples today.

The Anticipated
Peaceteacher

As the prophet Isaiah looked ahead to God's promised deliverer, his most poetic writing anticipated a Prince of Peace:

"For a child has been born to us, a son given to us; authority rests upon his shoulders; and he is named Wonderful Counselor, Mighty God, Everlasting Father, Prince of Peace. His authority shall grow continually and there shall be endless peace for the throne of David and his kingdom. He will establish it and uphold it with justice and with righteousness from this time onward and forevermore." (Isa 9:6-7)

"How beautiful upon the mountains are the feet of the messenger who announces peace, who brings good news, who announces salvation, who says to Zion, 'Your God reigns.'" (Isa 52:7)

God's Promised One will introduce shalom to all people. Isaiah's writings figured prominently in the memory of the Jewish people. It was only natural that this idea of the Messiah would be integral to the anticipation of Jesus' birth as recorded in the Gospel of Luke:

While the shepherds were keeping watch over their flocks by night outside Bethlehem, "suddenly there was with the angel a multitude of the heavenly host, praising God, and saying, "Glory to God in the highest heaven, and on earth peace among those whom he favors!" (2:14)

Jesus is introduced as the Prince of Peace in this birth narrative. The angels singing over the Bethlehem night foretold a forward-looking shalom, a shalom breaking into the world. It built upon Isaiah's earlier prophecy. When God's Promised One arrives, he will be a Prince of Peace, introducing God's Shalom to the earth. Isaiah's beautiful vision of a mountain messenger who brings the good news of shalom finds expression in the birth of Jesus in Bethlehem.

Peace is never a full reality in our lives or in our world because violence, disruption and war are always choices available to us. Peace is never a full reality in our homes because we choose violent words or actions toward our loved ones. Peace is no longer a full reality in our neighborhoods because we have become strangers to those next door. Peace is never a full reality between nations because we choose war and violence, injustice and division, revenge and retribution. There has never been a time in history when simultaneous wars have not been fought between nations or tribal groups.

If peace is to occur, it must be introduced into such a warring culture. We cannot wait until the time is right because the time for shalom is always now. The Peaceteacher said, "The Shalom of God is at hand." (Mk 1:15b) Seeds of peace must be planted and cultivated in our homes, neighborhoods, nations and globe. A vision of peace must be cherished in people's hearts and cultivated in people's minds. Isaiah planted and cultivated this vision for his people in exile: "I will appoint Peace as your overseer and Righteousness as your taskmaster. Violence shall no more be heard in our land, devastation or destruction within your borders." (Isa 60:17c-18a)

In the midst of warring madness, such a vision gives people hope of a better way, a brighter future, a time of shalom. Amidst the decadent and self-serving reign of King Herod, the severe Roman occupation and the compromised Jewish Temple hierarchy in Jerusalem, Jesus came as people were dreaming again of the birth of a Prince of Peace who would introduce God's shalom to the Jews and to the world.

We, too, live in a discouraging time when war serves as no real solution. World War I was fought as "the final war," the "war to end all wars," and establish lasting peace. It only led to World War II. World War II, "the good war," led to the Korean War, which led to the Cold War, which led to the Vietnam War, and now the War against Terror fought as actual wars in Iraq and Afghanistan. Nothing gets resolved. The Vietnam War was an American fiasco with many lost and wounded lives among the Vietnamese and the Americans. And yet America is again in another ill-defined war in Iraq, enflaming Islamic fundamentalists with little hope for a genuine exit strategy that would create a stable and independent nation.

This, like many ages before, is a discouraging time for peacemakers. With over 3,000 American soldiers who have returned home in body bags from the Iraqi War (as of 1/07), with an estimated 56,500 Vietnam War-era veterans and 18,500 Persian Gulf War-era veterans held in state and federal prisons (as of 1998, U.S. Dept of Justice), with 299,321 U.S. veterans homeless on any given night (National Coalition for Homeless Veterans), with 22,057 soldiers (as of 12/06) returning home wounded from the Iraq war, we are keenly aware of the high price of war.

Sometimes we must set our eyes ahead on a peace promised to us when in the present moment we see only violence, retribution and war. Jesus recognized that it is not easy to identify the signs of peace hidden in our current situation: "If you, even you, had only recognized on this day the things that make for peace! But now they are hidden from your eyes." (Lk 19:42) Perhaps the most brilliant aspect of Jesus' teaching about shalom is that it is breaking into this present moment as well as a vision of what can be in the future. So, it is at once both present and future. At some times in the present it is bold and obvious and other times barely noticeable. And some times in the future shalom seems so distant and other times there is such fervent hope for shalom. At those moments you feel as if you can reach out and touch it. So, for Jesus, shalom is both an attitude about the future and the ability to discern in the present moment. Walter Brueggemann states, "Shalom is rooted in a theology of hope, in the powerful, buoyant conviction that the world can and will be transformed and renewed, that life can and will be changed, and newness can and will come…(Shalom) is an announcement that God has a vision of how the world shall be and is not yet."[13]

Peace will break out here and there, and only becomes a full-fledged movement as people recognize peace and stand as its advocates. It requires a vision of shalom which counters personal and social realities. Peace must first be imagined in the minds and hearts of peacemakers before it becomes a social reality. Then it requires people working despite the evidence to make shalom happen. In this way peace nearly always subverts dominant and violent paradigms. While a typical response by individuals or nations is to be defensive, paranoid or belligerent, a peacemaker possesses a vision of shalom that paradoxically introduces forgiveness, reconciliation and harmony. The power of such a vision, a new way of seeing reality, must never be underestimated.

Jesus stressed that we must first see shalom around us even when it is subtle. Peacemakers see shalom when others cannot. "Once Jesus was asked by the Pharisees when the Shalom (kingdom) of God was coming, and he answered, 'The Shalom of God is not coming with things that can be observed; nor will they say, 'Look, here it is!' or 'There it is!' For, in fact, the Shalom of God is among you.'" (Lk 17:20-21) The Pharisees were devout and astute. They were looking for a fully-formed shalom in the future, not the present moment. However, the Shalom of God may not come in observable or flamboyant signs. It is, in fact, already around us if we have eyes to see it. Peacemakers ask, "Where is the Shalom of God around me? Where is it in my experience?"

Seekers of shalom ask these questions even in the midst of pain and madness.

Henri Nouwen writes, "...what makes us peacemakers is not threats or fears but the vision of the new and holy city coming down from heaven, the city of peace, the city without pain and agony, the city in which God will make his home among us. This vision is not a faraway utopian dream. It is a vision that is already being realized among us here and now in our Eucharistic community. It is a vision of the Lord-with-us in the midst of the sounds and spectacles of war. 'Happy are the eyes that see what you see,' Jesus says, 'for I tell you that many kings and prophets wanted to see what you see and never saw it.' (Lk 10:23-24) Thus our hope is based on what we already see, and what we see gives us always new courage to work for the day of the Lord when all powers of evil will be put under his feet and he will reign forever."[14]

In the summer of 2005, one mother of a soldier killed in Iraq, Cindy Sheehan, protested outside President Bush's ranch while he was there on vacation. It began as a solitary action to call for an end to a war with little justification in the first place and less justification to continue. But her vigil attracted global attention at a time when the President's approval ratings were at an all-time low due to the war. One can't predict what long-term impact such an action might have, but there is little doubt that she was motivated by shalom, a vision to make a difference for peace.

I am reminded of another peacemaker, Rachel Corrie, who as an American volunteer stood to her death in front of an U.S.-made Caterpillar tractor in a Palestinian village to stop punitive destruction of the home of a pharmacist. Rachel's courageous death began an international movement for peace.

There will always be those who say, "What's the use? I'm only one person. The obstacles to peace are so huge." And then there are peacemakers, filled with a vision, who cause peace to sprout forth from the earth amidst a barren landscape.

Isaiah prophesied, "Many peoples shall come and say, 'Come, let us go up to the mountain of the Lord, to the house of the God of Jacob; that he may teach us his ways, and that we may walk in his paths.' For out of Zion shall go forth instruction and the word of the Lord from Jerusalem. He shall judge between the nations, and shall arbitrate for many peoples; they shall beat their swords into plowshares, and their spears into pruning hooks; nation shall not lift up sword against nation, neither shall they learn war any more." (2:3-4) People must "learn war no more" but rather learn the ways of peace.

One should never underestimate the power of a shared vision to inspire people to claim the future. It is so easy to become beaten down by disappointment. It is easy to become apathetic. Jesus' vision was of a future kingdom "at hand," breaking in to this present moment. So it is not a far-off distant vision. It is a vision that begins in this present moment. It is a vision represented by every choice for shalom.

Martin Luther King, Jr. had a vision and often spoke of his dream, but he also saw his vision breaking into American society. He said on March 25, 1965, "We must come to see that the end we seek is a society at peace with itself, a society that can live with its conscience…I know you are asking today, 'How long will it take?' I come to say to you this afternoon however difficult the moment, however frustrating the hour, it will not be long, because truth pressed to earth will rise again.

"How long? Not long, because no lie can live forever.

"How long? Not long, because you still reap what you sow.

"How long? Not long. Because the arm of the moral universe is long but it bends toward justice.

"How long? Not long, because mine eyes have seen the glory of the coming of the Lord, trampling out the vintage where the grapes of wrath are stored. He has loosed the fateful lightning of his terrible swift sword. His truth is marching on…"[15]

Shalom comes as a gift. Jesus prayed, "Your kingdom come." (Mt 6:10a) He spoke of shalom coming to us. To receive it, we must have the openness of heart, mind and ear. Those with vision must recognize the need for shalom and recognize the small seeds of shalom sprouting in their midst. They must learn how to yearn for the coming Shalom of God, even when lacking tangible signs. They must yearn prior to an outbreak of shalom. They must participate in shalom even when barely recognized. All these things must be learned by a people and a culture that naturally seem to turn to violence, war and division. What is needed is a peaceteacher.

The Compassionate
Peaceteacher

We have little information about Jesus' first thirty years, presumably spent in Nazareth. We can assume that he experienced a growing sense of call to leave his mother and siblings and begin a public, itinerant ministry as a Jewish rabbi. Filled with a vision of God's shalom, he left the life he had known for the unfamiliar and unknown.

Jesus' "First Calling" was to teach others about the Shalom of God that he envisioned in his heart and articulated at the beginning of his ministry: "The Spirit of the Lord is upon me, because he has anointed me to bring good news to the poor. He has sent me to proclaim release to the captives and recovery of sight to the blind, to let the oppressed go free, to proclaim the year of the Lord's favor." (Lk 4:18-19, Isa 61:1-2) Isaiah summarized these passages with the exclamation, "For I, the Lord, love justice!" (61:8a)

This vision or calling is based on the in-breaking of

God's shalom. "The year of the Lord's favor" is the time acceptable or favorable to God. The time that God welcomes is best described by shalom. God welcomes shalom! Shalom is the time when captives are released, the blind receive sight, the oppressed go free, the poor receive good news, and justice prevails. Shalom is time pleasing to God.

In his first calling as a peaceteacher, Jesus told many parables. Some of these parables came to him from other rabbis and others were his own. His parables described the Shalom of God. He would ask, "To what can we compare the Shalom of God, or what parable will we use for it?" (Mk 4:30) And then he would tell a parable. (Mt 11:16, Mk 4:30, Lk 7:31, 13:18, 13:20) He became known so much for his parables that, over 2,000 years later, when parables are mentioned, people think of Jesus. He mastered the art as the parable-teller par excellence. It is hard to imagine another great teacher who so defines the category as Jesus does as parable-teller.

In Jesus' first calling as a peaceteacher, he focused upon the misery, suffering and pathos of others. His teaching ministry was interlaced with his healing ministry. The two were so intertwined that it is rare that he healed and didn't teach, or taught and didn't heal, thereby earning the title, **Compassionate Peaceteacher.**

Jesus' first calling is described in Matthew's Gospel: "Then Jesus went about all the cities and villages, teaching in their synagogues, and proclaiming the good news of the kingdom, and curing every disease and every sickness. When he saw the crowds, he had compassion for them, because they were harassed and helpless, like sheep without a shepherd." (Mt 9:35-36; see also Mt 14:14; 15:32; 20:34; Mk 8:2, 7:34; Lk 7:13) Healing and Teaching, Shalom and Wisdom, these were trademarks of the Compassionate Peaceteacher.

It was people and their predicaments, people and their sickness, that compelled him to heal and teach. His teaching was liberating and healing. His teaching gave new eyes to the blind, new ears to the deaf. He often gave "homework" (Mt 8:1-4; Mk 5:19-20; Lk 17:11-19; Jn 9:6-7) to those he healed. He suggested that their "faith-work" (Mt 8:5-13; 9:20-22; 9:27-29; 17:14-20; Mk 10:46-52) had everything to do with their healing. It wasn't just a matter of seeing with their eyes, but also seeing with their souls.

The movie, "At First Sight," features a stressed-out New York architect, Amy Benic, who went on vacation and fell in love with Virgil, a blind masseur. She learned through research that there might be a cure for his blindness, an experimental surgery that would allow Virgil to see the world as she saw it. At the end of the movie, successful eye surgery enabled Virgil to see for some period of time. Yet, gradually his retina disease returned, and he lost his sight. Throughout this time, he had been the object of much scientific interest, and Virgil spoke before a medical college where his surgery had been performed. Blind once again, Virgil said to them,

"Growing up blind, I had two dreams, one was to see, and the other was to play hockey for the NY Rangers. After the miracle of my brief period of sight, if I had to choose, I think I'd rather play hockey for the Rangers! It wasn't that seeing was so bad, and I saw lots of things and some were really beautiful and others were scary and some things I've already forgotten. A particular look in a pair of eyes, the clouds, those images will stay with me long after the light fades. As a blind man, I think that I see a lot better than I did when I was sighted-because I don't think we really see with our eyes. I think we live in darkness when we don't look at what's real about ourselves, about others and about life. I think no operation can do that. If you see what's real about yourself, you've seen a lot, and you don't need eyes for that."[16]

That's "Jesus Talk!" Look at the Gospels, and you will find Jesus turning the healed person so that she or he can further learn to be whole. (Mt 9:2-8; Mk 8:22-26; Lk 17:11-19; Jn 5:14; Jn 9:35-38) Continuously, he blessed those whom he healed with shalom. He wanted their specific healing to be accompanied by the wholeness of shalom. To the woman healed of the hemorrhage for 12 years he said, "Daughter, your faith has made you well; go in peace, and be healed of your disease." (Mk 5:34 and Lk 8:48) A woman who was a sinner entered the Pharisee's house and stood behind Jesus anointing him with oil. And Jesus said to the woman, "Your faith has saved you; go in peace." (Lk 7:50) Shalom was constantly on the lips of the Peaceteacher. It was his parting blessing to many whom he healed.

He sent out his disciples with instructions to remain in those homes where they found peace. (Mt 10:13) He once taught, "Salt is good, but if salt has lost its saltiness, how can you season it? Have salt in yourselves, and be at peace with one another." (Mk 9:50) He used the analogy of salt to urge his followers to live abundant and flavorful lives, but also to live at peace with others. What great wisdom! Live with flavor; live at peace.

Jesus taught people to organize their time around shalom. "Seek shalom first." (Mt 6:33) Seek shalom first, and everything will fall into place. Seek wholeness first. Seek the fulfillment of everyone first. Seek societal harmony first. Seek personal healing first. Seek reconciliation first. Seek the healing of the environment first. If it isn't shalom, don't put it first.

And Jesus prayed, "May shalom come on earth, O God, as in heaven." (Mt 6:10) May shalom come in my home, with my family, in my work, through my time, as in heaven. The Psalmist prayed, "This is the day that God has made, let us rejoice with shalom at its dawning." (118:24)

Jesus modeled how we are to receive shalom in the very heart of our being. As Jesus was baptized by John at the River Jordan, it was a shalom moment. When Jesus went into the wilderness after his baptism, though challenging and uncomfortable, it became a shalom moment. So often, Luke reported, "At daybreak, Jesus departed and went into a deserted place." (4:42; 5:16; 6:12; 9:10; 9:18; 9:28; 11:1) Jesus often sought his own shalom. At twelve years of age, he was found by his parents "listening to the teachers in the temple and asking them questions." (Lk 2:41) Luke spoke of how Jesus "increased in wisdom and in years, and in divine and human favor." (2:52) In Luke, nearly all of these opportunities when Jesus sought his own shalom occurred prior to setting "his face to go to Jerusalem." (9:51,53)

Jesus taught, "Blessed are the peacemakers." (Mt 5:9) He often taught about how to live as a peacemaker. "You have heard that it was said, 'An eye for an eye and a tooth for a tooth.' But I say to you, do not resist an evildoer. But if any-one strikes you on the right cheek, turn the other also..." Again, "You have heard that it was said, 'You shall love your neighbor and hate your enemy.' But I say to you, Love your enemies and pray for those who persecute you..." (Mt 6:38-44) He stressed the need for reconciliation: "So when you are offering your gift at the altar, if you are aware that your brother or sister has something against you, leave your gift there before the altar and go; first be reconciled to your brother or sister and then come and offer your gift." (Mt 5:23-24) He taught the importance of seeking one's own well-being: "Come to me, all you that are weary and are car-rying heavy burdens, and I will give you rest." (Mt. 11:28) As he restated the greatest commandments, he spoke of shalom-like relations with God, neighbor and self: "'You shall love the Lord your God with all your heart, and with all your soul, and with all your mind.' This is the greatest and first commandment. And a second is like it: 'You shall love your neighbor as yourself.' On these commandments hang all the law and the prophets." (Mt 22:37b-40)

It is during his years as compassionate peaceteacher that his many acts of healing are recorded. He constantly offered shalom to others. And when he healed, he often spoke of faith, forgiveness and courage.

Jesus as Confrontational Peaceteacher

Jesus taught that our allegiance must be to the Shalom of God and nothing else must stand in the way. The peace of which Jesus spoke has little to do with getting along or going along. Peace as complacency or disengagement was the opposite of what Jesus intended, and he boldly taught this when he said, "I came to bring fire to the earth, and how I wish it were already kindled! … Do you think that I have come to bring peace to the earth? No, I tell you, but rather division! From now on five members in one household will be divided, three against two and two against three; they will be divided: father against son and son against father, mother against daughter and daughter against mother…" (Lk 12:52-53) "Whoever loves father or mother more than me is not worthy of me…" (Mt 10:34) The Shalom of God must come first, before family, before parents, before comfort or security. Of what good are you to your family if you are not committed to the Shalom of God? You will only introduce strife and mistrust. Jesus once taught, "Whoever seeks the Shalom of God is my brother and sister and mother." (Mk 3:35) Seek shalom first. (Mt 6:33)

Jesus was a confrontational peaceteacher. A peaceteacher is not only meek and gentle, but also passionate and bold. The truth is that peace, just as war, must be waged. Peace is not only passive disengagement from violence and war, but also active engagement in nonviolent resistance, subversive teaching and prophetic call. Peace is waged with words and symbolic actions, often sharply confronting violence.

Martin Luther King, Jr. enraged many Americans with his proactive, nonviolent civil disobedience. King was particularly upset with moderate white clergy who failed to rise up against the injustice surrounding them. His famous, "Letter from a Birmingham City Jail," is addressed to white clergy. In it he confronts them saying, "...I came to Birmingham with the hope that the white religious leadership of this community would see the justice of our cause, and with deep moral concern, serve as the channel through which our just grievances would get to the power structure. I had hoped that each of you would understand. But again, I have been disappointed...I have watched white churches stand on the sideline and merely mouth pious irrelevancies and sanctimonious trivialities...So here we are moving toward the exit of the twentieth century with a religious community largely adjusted to the status quo, standing as a taillight behind other community agencies rather than a headlight leading men to higher levels of justice."[17]

One of the puzzling things about the Gospels is to discover what Jesus did that would have so threatened the Temple or Roman hierarchy to provoke his death. We know he often taught in a confrontational manner. In the Gospel of Luke there are fifty recorded teaching episodes in which Jesus confronted other rabbis, his disciples, or someone in the crowd, compared to thirty-nine non-confrontational teaching episodes. We have wanted Jesus to be innocent of any crime; yet there had to be something that provoked the ire of the authorities. The mere popularity of a Galilean rabbi would not have been enough.

John Dominic Crossan argues that it was Jesus' defiance in the Temple that brought on the hostility of the Temple leaders. What we call the cleansing or purification of the

Temple is misleading. Crossan believes it was more like "an attack, a destruction." He compares it to "going into a draft office during the Vietnam War and overturning drawers of file cards. It is symbolic negation of all that office or Temple stands for."[18] The Temple was led at that time by Roman appointees who were despised by most Jews. Jesus confronted them with the truth of their counterfeit leadership. Crossan says, "There is not a single hint that anyone was doing anything…inappropriate" in the Temple on the day Jesus drove out the moneychangers.[19] The moneychangers were exchanging coins so pious Jews could pay their Temple tax. Those who sold doves were in the Temple because Jewish infants were brought there, as was the baby Jesus, (Lk 2:23-24) to offer a sacrifice of "a pair of turtledoves or two young pigeons." By driving away the source of their income and by disrupting the sacrificial system, Jesus became an outrageous threat to the Temple leaders. Jesus had no issue with Temple worship; his issues were with its leaders whom he considered compromised and therefore illegitimate. James Charlesworth maintains that "Jesus was in conflict with the (Jewish) establishment, and his death may well be related to his attack against some of the sacerdotal aristocracy centered in Jerusalem and living in the palatial mansions on the western hill."[20]

Truth sometimes cuts. It often hurts, slicing through our comfortable worlds. The message of truth is simple: cut the hype, cut the pretense! Truth is what we don't want to hear. Facing the truth is always an awesome responsibility, a fearsome act.

Desmond Hoffmeister was a pastor in the coloured

township of Ennerdale near Johannesburg, South Africa. One of the tactics of the white apartheid government was to give enough privileges to the coloured population to turn them against the black majority. The apartheid government released Nelson Mandela around the time of my sabbatical in South Africa. We lived for one month in Ennerdale. Desmond invited Winnie Mandela to speak and share a meal with his small church in Ennerdale prior to a larger community rally. Not wanting the black ANC leader to bring trouble to Ennerdale, some residents began a wave of protests. Members left Desmond's small church, crippling its strength, but Desmond held his ground, and brought Ms. Mandela to Ennerdale to speak the truth in terms of what freedom meant to all South Africans, coloured, black, Afrikaner, Indian. This became a turning point in that township shedding its allegiance to apartheid.

The confrontational rabbi from Galilee flies in the face of the gentle Jesus, meek and mild. When the situation called for it, Jesus could be mild and gentle, but in reality, authorities don't put gentle teachers to death. They put peaceteachers, who confront the truth no matter the cost, to death.

Jesus as a confrontational teacher stood in a long prophetic tradition. The Jewish prophets were confrontational. They foretold what God was about to do, what people didn't want to hear. The prophet Amos thundered, "For three transgressions of Israel and for four, I will not revoke the punishment because you sell the righteous for silver, and the needy for a pair of sandals-you who trample the heads of the poor into the dust of the earth, and push the afflicted out of the way…Hear this word that the Lord has spoken against you, O people of Israel…" (2:6-7, 3:1)

Alice Franklin Bryant was living with her husband in the Philippines when the Japanese invaded during World War II. They kept moving inland to more remote locations, but eventually the Japanese found them and placed them in an internment camp. The conditions were deplorable, yet Alice always found humanity among her captors.

When the war ended, Alice returned home to Seattle and to the church I serve. She collected a book of letters from members of our church and from others who lived in Seattle. When she was paid a war reparation, she took the letters and the money and booked a trip to Hiroshima. She traveled around that region of Japan offering her apology for all the innocent families and children who had died or suffered because of the atomic bomb. Alice gave the funds to begin a community center to help meet the needs of the people made destitute by the war.

Alice was a persistent and life-long peace activist, often alienating others in our congregation and in the State of Washington who tired of her confrontational tactics and unpopular causes. Yet, near the end of her life, she was awarded an honorary key to the city of Seattle, and at the end of her life, the Washington State Legislature passed a resolution commending Alice's tireless peace advocacy. She was a confrontational peace activist who threw seekers of the status quo off their stride.

Jesus taught confrontationally. After the resurrection, Jesus confronted Peter three times, challenging his devotion and allegiance. He confronted the men who wanted to stone the woman caught in adultery. Jesus confronted Zacchaeus

(Lk 19:1f), Nicodemus (Jn 3:1f), the rich young ruler (Mt 19:16f), and those in his hometown synagogue. (Lk 4:16f)

The incident in the Nazareth synagogue is instructive of Jesus' confrontational style. After he read from the prophet Isaiah and declared this to be his life mission, "all spoke well of him and were amazed at the gracious words that came from his mouth." (Lk 4:22) But in his next words he reminded the Nazarenes that in the time of Elijah it was a Sidonite not a Jew who spared the nation from the famine. And during the time of Elisha, the only leper who was cleansed was a Syrian, while Israel was filled with lepers. This reminder that God's purposes are broader than the Jews enraged the entire synagogue, and they drove him away. Jesus taught that shalom is intended for everyone not just a few. It was a controversial teaching that alienated him from his hometown leaders.

Some may cite Jesus' harsh responses to the Pharisees and wonder if he truly was a peaceteacher. (Mt 15:7f) It is important to note that we are reading only one part of the dialogue. The Pharisees were Jesus' teachers. It was the nature of rabbinical debate to sharply hone arguments until the truth emerged. Sometimes peacemakers and peaceteachers appear to be picking a fight. They are not necessarily go-along, get-along people. What they are truly doing is placing choices squarely before people: peace and violence, life and death, conformity and subversity. They are forcing people to make a choice. (Deut 30:15f)

In the midst of my doctoral studies, my primary professor was sitting across his small office from me. Suddenly, he picked up a book and aimed it straight for my head. He intended to get my attention, and indeed he did. I will never forget the point he was making. I had written a paper in which I had argued that I was presenting a new idea. He wanted me to be more humble and aware of how much my "new idea" was borrowed or adapted. His aiming a book at my head was confrontational and effective. It left a deep impression, even though I ducked and he missed. Whenever I have claimed something to be new, I readily accept that it is also borrowed or adapted.

Jesus as confrontational peaceteacher leads to the next chapter in his life.

The Lenten Peaceteacher

Jesus was one of the greatest teachers in human history. And his greatest teaching happened toward the end of his life, when he revealed himself as the Lenten Peaceteacher.

Great teachers eventually realize that what they offer isn't the subject matter, their intellectual grasp, their latest technique or their impressive credentials. It's themselves. Great teachers don't pile information on top of their students. They get inside their students, and it's the same whether in the chemistry lab or the halls of poetry. Great teachers move from the object matter "out there" to the subject matter "in here." Jesus certainly made this journey as a peaceteacher.

Parker Palmer explained this idea in *The Courage to Teach:* "Teaching, like any truly human activity, emerges from one's inwardness, for better or for worse. As I teach, I project the condition of my soul onto my students, my subject, and our way of being together. ...teaching holds a mirror to the soul..."[21] "Bad teachers distance themselves from the subject they are teaching—and in the process, from their students. Good teachers join self and subject and students in the fabric of life."[22] My daughter had a college foreign language professor who told her, "I don't get paid enough to spend individual time with my students." Bad teacher. She didn't understand that she was the curriculum as much as the foreign language or the textbook. Walter Brueggeman states, "If you ask almost any adult about the impact of church school on his or her growth, he or she will not tell you about books or curriculum or Bible stories or anything like that. The central memory is of the teacher; learning is *meeting*."[23] I do not remember one thing Mrs. Weaver taught my unruly class of young boys in Sunday School. I will never forget the way her love calmed us and held us at rapt attention.

Jesus' second calling was to teach of himself to others. As the Lenten Peaceteacher, Jesus offered himself and God's Way for his life as his final parable. He became the parable of shalom, of fulfillment. He moved from the story of the Good Samaritan, of the Prodigal Son, of the woman searching for the lost coin, to the parable of the Son of Man who "must suffer and die." He continued the parabolic language from his era as Compassionate Peaceteacher.

The Lenten Peaceteacher became the curriculum. His own life and his own calling became the New Paradigm in which his followers could enter and learn. In this new calling, Jesus said, "Take my yoke upon you, and learn from me..." (Mt 11:29) Paul's letter to the Ephesians captured Jesus' Lenten calling when he wrote, "That is not the way you learned Christ." (4:20) The teacher and the subject matter become one and the same. You learn Christ as much as you learn *from* Christ.

It is his second calling as a teacher of shalom that made Jesus so different from other rabbis of first century Judaism, and so offensive to them. Rabbis did everything possible to "get out of the way" so that their singular focus was upon interpretation of the Law. They did not teach themselves, but the Torah. Other teachers said to Jesus, "You are testifying on your own behalf; your testimony is not true." (Jn 8:13-14) Jesus became the issue. He became the subject matter. When Jesus' life became his parable, his fellow teachers found this troublesome, even blasphemous.

In Matthew's Gospel, no conflict is reported between Jesus and other teachers until the ninth chapter. At that point, the conflicts centered on Jesus' teachings and his actions, not his identity. His own person did not become the issue until a mid-point return to his hometown. It was the Nazarenes in Matthew's Gospel of whom it was first said, "They took offense at him." (13:57a) In Matthew, as Jesus approached Jerusalem, he made himself the focus of his teaching. (16:13, 22:42, 26:11, 26:26)

In Mark's Gospel, others made Jesus the issue much earlier. (2:7, 3:7, 3:22, 6:1, 8:27) In Luke, it was the Devil (4:1) and unclean demons (4:34, 4:41, 8:28) who most often revealed Jesus' true identity, until Jesus himself began to make self-revelatory statements (7:23, 9:18), leading up to his Transfiguration. Jesus as the central issue came much earlier in the Gospel of John (1:29, 1:36, 1:49) and is pervasive throughout the fourth Gospel. However, whenever Jesus himself became the central issue, the conflict heightened with the authorities. The moment he turned toward Jerusalem and made his own passion the parable of his teaching, his death was inevitable.

At this point in Jesus' teaching there was a change of pace and locale. Jesus largely taught as the Compassionate Peaceteacher in his native Galilee. But as he "resolutely turned his face towards Jerusalem" (Lk 9:51), he taught as the Lenten Peaceteacher. The pace of Jesus' teaching intensified. "Then Jesus began to teach them that the Son of Man must undergo great suffering, and be rejected by the elders, the chief priests, and the scribes, and be killed, and after three days, rise again. He said all this quite openly." (Mk 8:31-32a) The Lenten Peaceteacher prophesied about the final passion of the Son of Man five times at mid-point in the Gospel of Matthew (16:21-23; 17:12; 17:22-23; 20:17-19; 26:2), and four times each in Mark (8:31-33; 9:12; 9:30-31; 10:32-34) and Luke. (9:22; 9:44-45; 17:24-25; 18:31-34)

Jesus was still teaching by parable. It is the "Son of Man" who must experience these things. The emphasis is now upon a new teaching. Mark wrote, "Then Jesus **began** to teach them..." (8:31) Matthew wrote, "**From that time on**, Jesus **began** to show his disciples that he must go to Jerusalem..." (16:21) Luke added emphasis, as Jesus said to his disciples, "Let these words sink into your ears: The Son of Man is going to be betrayed into human hands." (9:42)

The unusual aspect of this parable is that it was repeated multiple times in each of the synoptic Gospels and always as a private parable. Nearly all of Jesus' parables were taught publicly to crowds. This parable, all thirteen times, was told only to the disciples: "...he took the twelve disciples aside by themselves..." (Mt 20:17b) "...with only the disciples near him..." (Lk 9:18b) It might be called the Disciples' Parable.

The other emphasis of this parable is that it represents a new teaching. Six of the times the Son of Man Parable occurs in the Gospels, it specifically states that the disciples did not understand Jesus' words: "But they understood nothing about all these things; in fact, what he said was hidden from them, and they did not grasp what was said." (Lk 18:34) Luke reported, "They were afraid to ask him about this saying." (Lk 9:45c) Matthew reported that the disciples "were greatly distressed" (17:23c) after hearing Jesus tell this Son of Man parable. (see also Mark 9:32; 8:32; Mt 16:22) Mark reported that the disciples found Jesus' new parable to be offensive. "Peter took Jesus aside and began to rebuke him." (Mk 8:32b)

Jesus was frustrated with the inability of others, his followers and the crowds, to understand his vision of shalom. As Jesus approached Jerusalem, "he wept over it saying, 'If you, even you, had only recognized on this day the things that make for peace! But now they are hidden from your eyes.'" (Lk 19:41-42)

This is a new teaching by a rabbi transforming himself, his role, and the content of his teaching midpoint in his rabbinical career. The disciples had a hard time letting go of the Compassionate Peaceteacher and accepting Jesus as the Lenten Peaceteacher. One wonders why the parable is repeated five times in Matthew and four times each in Luke and Mark. Of course, it is a literary technique by the Gospel writers to emphasize its importance. Also, good teachers repeat a lesson when it proves difficult for students to understand.

To fully understand this parable, we must understand the expression, "Son of Man," which has roots in Hebrew scripture, notably Ezekiel, Daniel and in apocryphal writings. It is an important expression in the Gospels as they "repeatedly depict Jesus using the expression 'the son of the man,' as virtually his only form of self-reference. Not once in the Gospels does he call himself by his own name. Not once does anyone else call him the son of the man. The expression appears only on his lips."[24] The phrase appears eighty-seven times in the four Gospels. Walter Wink points out that "In Hebrew the phrase simply means 'a human being.'"[25] The Son of Man speaks of Jesus' mission of shalom, of helping people become more fully human, more whole, more fulfilled. The Son of Man speaks of Jesus embodying shalom. The Son of Man could be called the Person of Shalom.

Jesus first told the Son of Man parable in all three Synoptic Gospels just after Peter identified Jesus as the Messiah. Such placement of the parable draws out its messianic roots. Like many of Jesus' parables, the Son of Man parable is typically one sentence: "Jesus said to them, 'The Son of Man is going to be betrayed into human hands, and they will kill him, and on the third day he will be raised.'" (Mt 17:22-23a) The Son of Man is an ambiguous term, perfectly suited for a parable by Jesus. It leaves the hearer with several questions: Was Jesus speaking of himself or another? Was he claiming a messianic role for himself or another? Was he prophesying his own future or something else?

Jesus' parables always left the hearer with the task of interpretation. It is the language of metaphor, not description. The incredible future knowledge ascribed to Jesus regarding his own destiny must not sidetrack us. The first telling by Jesus of this parable is found in Luke 9: "The Son of Man is going to be betrayed into the hands of men." It isn't hard to imagine that Jesus must have known where his challenge to the authorities would lead, nor how predictably hard it would be for his disciples to accept.

In his calling as the Lenten Peaceteacher, it wasn't the pathos of others as much as his own impending passion that became the primary focus. Once Jesus prophesied his death for the final time, only one remaining healing is reported in the Gospels of Matthew and Luke. (Mt. 20:30-34 & Lk. 18:35-43) In the Gospel of Mark, only one healing is reported after Jesus first prophesied his impending death. (Mk 10:46-52) Jesus' healings are basically over by this point. His curriculum and focus have changed.

Two events seem to issue forth his Second Calling as a peaceteacher. One was the death of John the Baptist. John was a forerunner, a mentor, and to some extent, Jesus' teacher. John's cruel fate surely awakened Jesus as to the likelihood of his own impending death and the eventuality of God's design for his life. When Jesus received the news of John's beheading by Herod, "he withdrew by boat to a lonely place where they (he and the Twelve) could be by themselves." (Mt. 14:13)

The second event which prompted Jesus' Second Calling as a peaceteacher was Peter's confession that Jesus was the Messiah, the Christ. (Jn. 6:67-71; Lk. 9:18-21; Mk.

8:27-30; Mt. 16:13-20) In all four Gospels, Peter's confession immediately preceded Jesus turning toward Jerusalem, and in all three Synoptic Gospels, it immediately preceded the first time he taught his disciples about his own fate using the Person of Shalom (Son of Man) parable. It was as if his disciples had to grasp who he was before he could reveal to them his ultimate destiny.

Jesus as Lenten Peaceteacher fully opened himself to his disciples and in so doing evidenced his greatest teaching. As memorable as was his Sermon on the Mount or Beatitudes or his parables, it was his Person of Shalom (Son of Man) parable that changed the world.

Great teaching is always revelatory. If the teacher is closed and guarded, little learning occurs. Teaching is more soul-work than memory-work. It's transformational more than informational. It reveals the teacher and students at the core, at the same time revealing the truth of what is being pursued or explored.

As Lenten Peaceteacher, Jesus was so revelatory with his students that at first they couldn't understand or connect. They were frightened when he revealed that much of himself. Only in glimpses do we see his disciples reveal as much in return. One example was when Thomas urged the other disciples to return to Judea with Jesus knowing full well that it would be at risk of death. Thomas said, "Let us also go, that we may die with him." (John 11:16b) Another example was at Simon's house in Bethany when a woman came to Jesus and began preparing his body for burial, though he was still alive. She, far ahead of the other disciples, understood Jesus' fate. And he commended her for her heroic act. (Mt. 26:6-13)

Jesus' words and teaching must have become clearer to

his disciples when the parable came to reality in their first-hand experience of Jesus' death and resurrection. Jesus' prophetic passion declarations, as offered in the Synoptic Gospels, laid the groundwork far in advance of the disciples' capability to understand at the time. Jesus, the Lenten Peaceteacher, could only hope that these passion declarations were adequate for his disciples to lay claim to his most self-revelatory teaching and boldly declare the parable of his crucifixion and resurrection to a waiting world.

The ultimate challenge of shalom is a willingness to give one's life to it. It is the price so many peaceteachers such as Gandhi, Martin Luther King, Jr, Dietrich Bonhoeffer, and more recently, Rachel Corrie, have paid. Each of these peaceteachers could have cried out with the Psalmist, "For too long have I had my dwelling among those who hate peace. I am for peace, but when I speak, others are for violence." (120:6-7)

One of the former pastors of the church I serve saw the savagery of war during World War I. He left military service deeply disillusioned. He eventually became an avowed pacifist determined to use his influence to prevent a repetition of armed conflict. Rumors were spread that Dr. Elmer Fridell was a communist. One member recalled that one Sunday the congregation was startled with Dr. Fridell's revelation that "we have in our congregation today, as we have had in Sundays past, officers of the Army in plain clothes to observe and listen, for they do not like that I preach peace."

Sometimes we are called to risk our reputation, to suffer unfair accusations, or to face criticism and ridicule, all because we follow the peaceteacher who shows us the way of shalom. Jesus knew that we must each "take up our cross" if we are to embrace shalom. There is no other way.

The Resurrected Peaceteacher

Jesus' revelatory teaching as the Lenten Peaceteacher came to fruition in the resurrection. Jesus not only taught shalom, he himself became the Shalom of God. Christian scriptures state that this was the role God intended all along. Jesus' journey of faith was completed with the transformation that occurred through the crucifixion and resurrection. In that torturous crucible, he became the Shalom of God.

It is not his role alone, though the crucified and resurrected Christ is the fullest revelation of the Shalom of God. If Jesus were the only human being to become shalom, then his life would be novel, but somewhat irrelevant to ours. We are also called not only to receive shalom, but to be shalom. I have been privileged to know a few people who, well into their earthly pilgrimages, have slowly been transformed into shalom. As the old gospel hymn states, "more like Jesus would I be."

One person who became shalom to me was Emma Lou Benignus. Emma Lou taught me how to meditate and pray with my entire body when I was in my early 30's and ten years into pastoral ministry. She was a wise sage, my peaceteacher. Her deep, personal interest in me was transformational. Emma Lou had an eager mind, a love for learning, and a capacity for interacting around great theological ideas. Whenever I visited her apartment, I would scour her cluttered living room examining carefully the books she was reading. They immediately entered my reading list. Emma Lou was a theologian and seminary professor who eschewed degrees and titles. She was never self-promotional but always self-respectful. There was nothing pretentious about her; she was utterly human. Once, I introduced her to my congregation as "Dr. Benignus", and she gently reminded me that it wasn't the title but the substance that mattered. She was right. It was her substance, her peaceful manner, her passion for shalom, that gently transformed her into shalom. She spoke of this as the power of God recreating us into a "New Humanity." Her shalom was a blessing in my life.

Yet, for me, becoming shalom seems utterly out of reach. How do we live for shalom when peace is so illusive in our world? How do we hope for fulfillment when our lives and our society are so broken? How do we overcome disillusionment with our seeming disposition toward competition, violence and conflict? In the final chapter of Jesus' calling as peaceteacher, he offered five Shalom Learnings:

First, we cannot go part of the way but the whole way with the Peaceteacher. Partway ends at Palm Sunday, or

Maundy Thursday, or even Good Friday. None of those are good ending places. If we end on Palm Sunday, we have but a new chapter in a triumphal, nationalistic faith. If we end on Maundy Thursday, we are left with a threatened faith. If we end on Good Friday, we have a defeated faith. Only Easter offers hope. We have to go the whole distance with God to become shalom.

I have preached many sermons around the three questions posed by the resurrected Jesus to Peter, "Do you love me?" (Jn 21:15f.), but I have never preached a sermon on Jesus repeating the message, "Shalom be with you." (Jn 20:19d; 20:21a) It could be simple redundancy, but I think there may be a reason for the repetition in the same discourse. When Jesus appeared to his disciples "on the evening of the first day of the week," he greeted them saying, "Shalom be with you." This was a customary Jewish greeting in the first century. He could also have been reminding his disciples of his earlier teaching, "Shalom I leave you; my shalom I give to you." (Jn 14:27a) Shalom is a gift we are to receive. We are to become shalom by receiving shalom.

However, Jesus repeated the same message in the next sentence, "Again Jesus said, 'Shalom be with you! As the Father has sent me, I am sending you.'" (Jn 20:21; see also Jn 17:18) His message no longer emphasized the gift but the mission of shalom. As the resurrected Christ, Jesus doesn't offer a half-way message. He goes the whole way, urging us to receive shalom first and then go forth with shalom as our mission. We are to **receive shalom** and **strive for shalom**. The next verse is even more instructive, "When he said this, he breathed on them and said to them, 'Receive the Holy

Spirit. If you forgive the sins of any, they are forgiven them..." (20:22a) This is the only place in the New Testament where the verb "to breathe" occurs, and it speaks of the inbreathing of the Spirit of God upon the disciples as they go out with shalom on their hands and in their voices. His mandate, "Shalom be with you," is an empowering message to take the power of the Holy Spirit and the power of forgiveness into the world. The world is to become shalom by our sharing it through the inbreathing power of the Spirit of God.

Second, at 'in-between' places, shalom will appear illusive. It is easy to think of shalom as the absence of suffering. Yet, for Jesus, shalom so fulfilled his life-purpose that it deserved his suffering and even his death. Along the way of shalom, there will be defeats and losses for all of us. The more boldly we advocate for shalom, the greater the opposition we will face. The fact that we can't easily recognize shalom does not mean it is absent.

During World War II, the church I serve had another pacifist pastor. During this time there was a widespread mistrust of the Japanese even though Seattle had a long established population of Japanese Americans. Dr. Harold Jensen urged our members to ignore a public boycott of Japanese businesses and patronize their stores. Twelve young people in the church volunteered their blood for a Japanese American hospital patient. Fifteen cars from the church helped with transportation when the evacuation began forcibly removing the Japanese from Seattle. When the Japanese were sent off to internment camps and their property was seized, Dr. Jensen led members of the congregation to store household items for the Japanese, and it is even rumored that some items were stored in our church building. All of this was viewed as aiding and abetting the enemy. He followed the Japanese to Puyallup where they were first taken and held a service of communion prior to their being sent to more remote camps. His efforts would have been viewed by most as un-American. I can't imagine that Dr. Jensen and others who agreed with him could have recognized shalom in those tragic days amidst such injustice to innocent Americans. They had to recognize that they were living in an "in-between" time, when shalom seemed remote and injustice had overtaken society.

Third, define shalom carefully. We must take care not to define shalom in purely self-centered ways. Shalom includes inner peace but it also includes shalom for everyone. Shalom has nothing to do with self-gain at the expense of others. Shalom requires stirring the water, jarring our complacency, upsetting our assumptions, and capsizing our prejudices. Peace often comes after we have been disturbed. It may not feel like shalom even though we are on the path toward its realization. When white people care about racial equality, when straight people care about marriage equality, when Christians care about anti-Semitism, when men care about feminism, when people care passionately about causes for which there is no immediate self-gain, then you can trust this to be the way of shalom.

It is possible to be an angry peacemaker. It is possible to be a militant, strident, fanatical peacemaker. I have known some people who advocate for peace in un-peaceful ways. I have seen this tendency in myself when I approach peace-making by creating categories of "us" and "them." The language at most public peace rallies has to do with bashing the opinions and integrity of those who disagree. The applause is louder when the speaker becomes more militant. Shalom is a stronger word than peace, because you can't angrily seek shalom. You can't approach shalom stridently. Shalom by definition includes your well-being and that of an enemy, stranger or friend. If we define shalom carefully, it includes personal wholeness and health for every person and for all of society.

Fourth, recognize the difference between a momentary experience of shalom and the long-anticipated arrival of shalom filling every crevice of the earth. Our work as peacemakers is not done until the earth is filled with shalom. Nearly all of the Hebrew prophets foretold such a time. Ezekiel prophesied, "I will make a covenant of peace with them; it shall be an everlasting covenant with them; and I will bless them and multiply them, and will set my sanctuary among them forevermore." (37:26) Even with this future anticipation, it is important to recognize momentary experiences of shalom in the present moment. A momentary experience of shalom is a step toward the fullness that shalom represents. Often it is our own awakening that occurs in small steps.

I met Beyers Naude in South Africa when he was an elder statesman of post-apartheid South Africa. He began his adult life as an Afrikaner pastor and member of the

Broederbond, a secret society dedicated to the preservation of apartheid and Afrikaner dominance in South African society. Slowly, his eyes were opened. In an early experience, Beyers was horrified by his ignorance of his own country. "I realized I had been living in a wonderful 'white world.' And right next to me was a black world and a brown world and an Indian world that I knew nothing about."[26] From that point on, a new idea began to take root in his mind. Eventually Naude was rejected by his church and government and was forced to live under house arrest when he was banned for seven years. All contact with the public was prohibited by the government. Yet, from his early glimpses of shalom for all people in his society, he emerged from his banning order with a deeper vision for the fullness of shalom. After becoming general secretary of the South African Council of Churches and once again in public life, "Beyers never changed his view that violence was wrong and counter-productive, but he believed the conflict was the inevitable result of apartheid and he refused to judge those who had taken up arms against white rule. But he also believed that there was no turning back from a new South Africa and that its people would finally be forced to resolve their differences around the conference table...At a time when government propaganda against the African National Congress reached its height, Naude threw his considerable influence behind the drive for negotiations and meetings with the ANC...He was uncompromising in his support for black initiatives."[27] Naude played a key role in the peaceful transition to black majority rule in South Africa. His was a journey from his first, momentary glimpses of shalom until he himself became the shalom that South African society so desperately needed.

Fifth, shalom is God's gift and God's action. God is the true Peacemaker and we are peacehelpers. We have a role to play, but there is always something larger at work. God's gift to the world is shalom, and God's presence permeating all of creation is shalom. Peacehelpers do not have to be tormented by the burden of shalom depending solely upon us. It doesn't all fall on our shoulders. A tormented peacemaker is an oxymoron! When it came time to build a magnificent Temple in Jerusalem, the word of God came to David, "You have shed much blood and have waged great wars; you shall not build a house to my name…See, a son shall be born to you; he shall be a man of peace. I will give him peace from all his enemies on every side;…and I will give shalom and quiet to Israel in his days." (I Chronicles 22:8f.) Shalom is God's gift. We are called to be peacehelpers, but shalom comes in God's time and in God's own way.

Sometimes as a pastor, I have had a difficult time drawing boundaries around my desire to help people. I recall once when very close friends were having marital difficulties, I became not only their pastor, their best friend, but also their marital counselor. It became my intense desire to "save" their marriage. I counseled both of them individually and as a couple. In my attempts to help them hear the other, I became a go-between passing messages back and forth. I met with their children to help them understand the challenge their parents experienced. My savior complex was out of control and if I hadn't backed off, I am convinced that shalom would not have returned to this family. If I had persisted in playing all these conflicting roles, I would have become part of the problem instead of the solution. Shalom is God's gift. I can help shalom but it is God's gift, not mine.

In a Mountain Classroom

Twice in Matthew's account of the resurrection, the women who came to the empty tomb were told to tell the other disciples: "Go to Galilee; there they will see him." (28:7) Later, we read, "Now the eleven disciples went to Galilee, to the mountain to which Jesus had directed them." (28:16) Earlier, but still near the end of his life, Jesus told his disciples, "After I am raised up, I will go ahead of you to Galilee." (Mt 26:32) One is reminded of a mountain in Galilee that served as the setting for the Sermon on the Mount. (Mt 5:1) Or the Mount of the Transfiguration, where Jesus took Peter, James and John to more fully reveal himself. (Mt 17:1) It is to the Galilean mountains that Jesus went to pray (Mt 14:23; Lk6:12), to be by himself (Mk 6:46), to withdraw with his disciples. Jesus is often reported as having come down from the mountain, presumably by himself, or with his inner circle. (Mt 8:1) On a mountain overlooking the Sea of Galilee, Jesus sat down, and great crowds came to him, and he healed many. (Mt 15:29) It was on that mountain that the miracle of the multiplication of the loaves and fishes occurred. (Mt 15:32f.) In Mark's Gospel, it was on a mountain where Jesus appointed twelve to be his disciples. (3:13)

Jesus' "classroom" with his inner circle of disciples tended to be in the mountains, away from the crowds, where they would not be interrupted. Jesus' retreat for spiritual renewal was in the mountains, and when the angel appeared to the women in the garden, the angel directed them to tell the disciples to go to a mountain in Galilee and there they would see him, the Risen Peaceteacher. As the women raced from the Garden, the Resurrected Jesus greeted them, repeating the angel's message: "Go and tell my brothers to go to Galilee; there they will see me." (Mt 28:10)

Clearly, Jesus was no longer the Lenten Peaceteacher, no longer suffering on his journey to death. Now, he had become the Resurrected Peaceteacher, and yet he still met his disciples "in the classroom," in the mountains, where he shaped them once again into the community he needed them to be.

But, you can't meet the Resurrected Peaceteacher on the mountaintop unless you first journey through the valley with the Lenten Peaceteacher. It's not a cheap or momentary victory. It requires a willingness to suffer and sacrifice. If you walk through Lent, while you may not feel victorious, the Peaceteacher will meet you someday on the mountaintop, and just as with his first disciples, you will find shalom. Peace is introduced as we are willing to pay the price and endure the sacrifice for the Shalom of God, not just for ourselves, but for the world. By this standard, Jesus was the ultimate peaceteacher because he was willing to pay the price and endure the ultimate sacrifice to become God's shalom in the world.

It is interesting that Jesus greeted his followers as the resurrected Lord with the word, "shalom." "While the disciples were talking, Jesus himself stood among them and said to them, 'Shalom be with you.'" (Lk 24:36; Jn 20:19) Jesus again said to them, "Shalom be with you." (Jn 20:21) A week later his disciples were again in the house and although the doors were shut, Jesus came and stood among them and said, "Shalom be with you." (Jn 20:26) In John, Jesus spoke of his impending departure from his disciples and his ministry when he said, "Shalom I leave with you; my shalom I give to you. I do not give to you as the world gives. Do not let your hearts be troubled, and do not let them be afraid." (Jn 14: 27) "The hour is coming, indeed it has come, when you will be scattered, each one to his home, and you will leave me alone. Yet, I am not alone because the Father is with me. I have said this to you, so that in me you may have shalom." (Jn 16:31-33a)

Even after his death, Jesus was a peaceteacher of shalom in his resurrection appearances with his followers.

Jesus' Way of Shalom

The most traditional formula for becoming a Christian is that you are a sinner, separated from God. Jesus died for your sins. If you confess your sins, you can be reunited with God and have the gift of eternal life.

For many people, this formula still works. For other seekers, it is lacking because they are already burdened with shame, guilt and low self-esteem. They do not find themselves attracted to a faith that requires them to begin as a sinner. Secondly, many people find it hard to relate to a God from whom separation is a given. Many now relate to God as Being or Presence or Spirit who is within and above and around. For such an understanding, it doesn't make sense to begin with separation. This doesn't call for a rejection of Christianity, but rather a reformulation of Jesus' way of shalom. In addition to saying, "Jesus died for our sins", it can be said another way.

Jesus lived, died and rose from the dead:

- for our fulfillment. We can walk Jesus' way of shalom with confidence that, like Jesus, we can participate in the Shalom of God;
- so that we would never be ultimately defeated or discouraged by the un-shalom-like nature of the world and our lives;
- so that we would not have to fear death. We know that the world cannot overcome or overwhelm the love of God. God's love is ultimate and eternal;
- to release us from the burden of the Shalom of God falling fully upon our shoulders. Shalom comes from God and God has the final Word. Shalom is ultimately "God's doing."

Jesus' way of shalom follows the teaching chapters in his life:

A. Vision: The beginning of faith is envisioning the possibilities of shalom.

How can your call, your potentiality, your dreams, your vision, your meaning in life, center around shalom? You are called to receive shalom, but you cannot receive it unless you can first envision it. Can you envision shalom in your life? Can you envision shalom in your neighborhood, your city, your nation, between nations?

(The Anticipated Peaceteacher)

B. Wholeness: **Jesus' way of shalom leads toward healing of self and others.** Shalom leads to the discovery of wholeness in your life and in the lives of all others, including foreigners, strangers and enemies. You are called to introduce wholeness in your community. In this way, you engage in the work of shalom and introduce shalom to others. *What could wholeness look like in your life? In your body? In your lifestyle? In your choices? In your values? In your actions? How can you be an instrument of shalom for others and for the world?* **(The Compassionate Peaceteacher)**

C. Sacrifice: **Jesus' way of shalom requires a willingness to take risks and make sacrifices.** *What risks will shalom require of you? What sacrifices? What price are you willing to pay to introduce shalom to the world?* **(The Lenten Peaceteacher)**

D. Fulfillment: **Jesus' way of shalom offers the promise of fulfillment in this life and in a life that transcends death.** Your vision of shalom ultimately reaches fruition. *Can you recognize fulfillment breaking forth in your life? Does the future promise of shalom encourage you to live for today? Whenever peace breaks out anywhere, can you see this as a sign of a coming shalom? Can you see a partial fulfillment of shalom in your life or in the world as a blessing from God?* **(The Resurrected Peaceteacher)**

Jesus as Peaceteacher offers his followers vision, wholeness, sacrifice and fulfillment as the way to the Shalom of

God for individuals and the world.

Vision, Wholeness, Sacrifice and Fulfillment were sequential phases in Jesus' path of shalom for peace, even though they may not be sequential for us. Often, they co-mingle throughout our lives. There are times when we are seeking wholeness for others and times when we are envisioning the possibilities of shalom. There are times when we receive the fruits of shalom, even fleetingly, but it is Jesus' way of shalom that includes sacrifice and risk, wholeness and fulfillment. Those who follow the way of shalom "shall go out in joy, and be led back in peace, the mountains and the hills before you shall burst into song, and all the trees of the field shall clap their hands." (Isa 55:12) This is the Gospel of Shalom of which the Apostle Paul wrote, "put on whatever will make you ready to proclaim the gospel of peace." (Eph 6:15)

We are never left on our own as we follow the way of shalom. We have a Peaceteacher who shows us the way.

Postcript One:
Breathing Shalom

I am filled with fear, with regret, with reluctance,
with worry.
Fill me with your shalom, O God.
May your shalom overtake me
from the top of my head to the bottom of my feet.
May your gentle shalom ease the tension
that creases my forehead
and causes me to lie awake at night.
May I breathe shalom.

My relationships are not what I want them to be.
I am surrounded by people from morning to night,
yet I maintain distance.
Fill me with your shalom, O God.
May your shalom ease the distance
and overcome the isolation
within my community of friends
and among my loved ones and neighbors.
May we breathe shalom together.

This world is filled with the madness of violence,
the insanity of revenge, the stupidity of war.
This world is filled with polarized neighbors
pulling against each other.

I participate in the polarization.
I further "for" and "against."
May your shalom ease the misunderstanding
and the fear that fuel war, violence and prejudice.
May your shalom overtake nations and world leaders.
May your shalom give me back my voice of conscience,
my passion for justice, my commitment to nonviolence.
May the world breathe shalom.

May I be your shalom in my family, among my friends,
within my community of faith,
in my vocation and in the world.
And when I fail, may your shalom embrace my weakness
so that I learn to breathe shalom once again.

Postscript Two:
Re-Telling Jesus' Early Ministry Years

When Jesus was around 30 years of age, he left his mother and siblings and his home village of Nazareth. He felt compelled to seek God's shalom, and he set out to find the voice of one crying in the wilderness, "Prepare the way of the Lord." John the Baptist appeared in the wilderness preaching, "After me comes he who is greater than I. I baptize you with water, but he will immerse you with the Shalom of God."

In those days Jesus came from Nazareth and was baptized by John in the Jordan River. And when Jesus came up out of the water, immediately the heavens opened and the Spirit descended upon him like a dove, and a voice spoke, "You shall be my shalom to all people."

Immediately Jesus left John the Baptist and went into the wilderness. And he was purified by the experience and came out with a new calling from God at the heart of his being. From that moment on, the Shalom of God was first in his life.

Jesus returned to Galilee, preaching, "Repent, for the time is fulfilled, and the Shalom of God is at hand." And passing along the Sea of Galilee, he saw Simon and Andrew casting a net into the sea, for they were fishermen. And Jesus said to them, "Follow me and I will make you fishers of shalom." And they left their nets and followed him.

With his new disciples behind him, Jesus began to proclaim, "Behold, the Shalom of God has come near." Jesus went throughout Galilee, teaching in the synagogues and healing every disease and sickness among the people. For he had great compassion on the crowds, and yearned that each person he met had God's gift of healing and wholeness.

Once, he went up to the mountain and he taught them saying, "Blessed are the meek, for they will inherit the earth. Blessed are the merciful, for they will receive mercy. Blessed are the peacemakers, for they will be called children of God. Blessed are the poor, for theirs is the Shalom of God." He continued teaching, "You are the light of the world. A city built on a hill cannot be hid. Do not hide the light of shalom from the world. Indeed, in everything, do not worry about your physical needs, but seek shalom first and all other things will be added to you.

"You have heard it said of ancient times, 'You shall not murder,' but I say to you that if you are angry with a brother or sister, or insult a brother or sister, you violate shalom. You have heard it said, 'An eye for an eye and a tooth for a tooth,' but I say to you, 'If anyone strikes you on the right cheek, offer him the other also. Do not resist an evildoer.' You have heard it said, 'Love your neighbor and hate your enemy.' But I say to you, 'Love your enemies and pray for those who persecute you.' In all these ways, seek shalom first."

"Pray with these words, 'Our God in heaven, holy is your name. May your shalom come on earth as in heaven.' Not everyone who says to me, 'Lord, Lord,' will enter the Shalom of God, but only the peacemakers."

Jesus once said to them, "I have not come to you preaching complacency or comfort. Peace comes like a storm, capsizing the status quo, forcing you to choose shalom above everything else, even family relations or loyalty to the kingdoms of this world."

Again he said, "Welcome everyone. For as you welcome the stranger, you welcome me. Be compassionate to everyone, for as you show mercy to the stranger, you show mercy to me. Do not judge others."

He once said to teachers of the law standing nearby, "Woe to you! For you tithe mint and rue and herbs of all kinds, but you neglect justice and shalom. How difficult it will be for a rich person to receive the Shalom of God."

Once Jesus was asked, "When is the Shalom of God coming?" He answered, "It is not coming in obvious ways that can be observed. For, in fact, it is already among you."

And the crowds were astonished at his teaching for he appeared as one filled with the Shalom of God. He lived the life he taught.

Postscript Three:
The Asian Teacher

We might better envision Jesus as Peaceteacher outside our own cultural context. Trapped within our cultural boundary, it becomes difficult to view Jesus through a different lens.

It may be argued that Jesus is the most dominant figure in western history, having literally changed our dating of time from his birth. He has influenced every facet of western civilization, from art to science to politics. That is not to say that the mentality of people from the United States or Europe more closely resembles that of Jesus. There is far too much greed and violence in western society for that to be true.

Jesus is traditionally viewed by the church through Pauline eyes. The Apostle Paul brought the church westward from rural Palestinian and Galilean roots into the Greek and Roman cities of the first century. This was true to the extent the conclusion must be drawn that Paul either knew very little of those rural Palestinian roots, or he ignored them in his writing and ministry.

This is all the more fascinating given the fact that Jesus was born in Asia. Turkey is Asia Minor and Jesus was born even further from the continent of Europe. The Gospel of Matthew claims that he spent part of his childhood in Africa as a refugee with his parents. (Mt 2:14) It also claims that his birth was honored by three Asian sages from the East who practiced Persian astrology. (Mt 2:1f)

New Testament scholars have helped us see that the four Gospels were directed to the western churches that Paul and others founded, and are documents intended as good news to those people. Paul and Timothy "went through the region of Phyrgia and Galatia, having been forbidden by the Holy Spirit to speak the word in Asia." (Acts 16:6; Asia here refers to SW part of Asia Minor) If the Gospels had been written to churches founded by missionaries and evangelists in Armenia, the tenor of the Gospels would have been remarkably different. And that is not so preposterous because the Roman World of the first century extended into Armenia and Mesopotamia. Major trading occurred in this era between India and the Roman Empire with significant Jewish populations living along the coast of India. Paul headed toward the center of the empire, not to its edges, and within 300 years, his strategy proved successful when the entire Empire turned toward Christianity, a development that would have seemed inconceivable to Paul or anyone else in the first century.

The Christian Testament from cover to cover is addressed to Europeans. It is their first century urban context and the Roman Empire of the Northern Mediterranean world that is the focus of each New Testament author. While Paul spent a great deal of time in Asia Minor, he focused almost exclusively on the Hellenized cities of that region, cities turned toward the West, not the East. Bernard Lee states, "a Jewish sense of things early gave way to a rather more Greek sense of things as a framework for interpreting the meaning of Jesus...The Palestinian Jewish road, became the far less traveled road."[28]

Consider how different it would be if the Christian Testament was addressed exclusively to Asians! Jesus' ministry was largely limited to Asians. As far as we know, he didn't mix often with Greeks or Romans, nor did he often travel to the Greek and Roman cities that surrounded him throughout his ministry. He even said, "I was sent only to the lost sheep of the house of Israel." (Mt 15:24) He kept to his Asian context and never left it on foot or in heart. He was more Palestinian and Galilean than the cosmopolitan Jews who had become Hellenized. What is remarkable is that even though the four Gospels retold the story of Jesus' life for Europeans, they nevertheless offer us a somewhat revealing picture of Jesus' Asian roots. They tell his story in Galilean context, sometimes explaining the Jewishness of Jesus to their European/Gentile audience. (e.g., Lk 20:27; Jn 4:9, 19:31, 40) Once, in Matthew's Gospel, he describes how Jesus' "fame spread throughout all Syria…" (4:24) His fame was reaching further into Asia.

When the evangelists and missionaries took the Gospel to the Europeans, they didn't deem it appropriate to call Jesus a teacher. It is hardly mentioned in any of Paul's writings or other canonical letters. This is peculiar because the role of teacher in Greek culture was highly valued. One might think that reminding the Greeks that Jesus was a wise Jewish sage would have been compelling. Instead, they called him "savior and lord," politically charged terms restricted in the first century to describe Roman Emperors. They went right to the heart of the matter, challenging the principalities and powers of the Mediterranean Empire. Yet, they also left behind an important part of Jesus' Asian identity.

Jesus was an Asian peaceteacher, standing in a relatively new Jewish tradition dating from the beginning of the

Hellenistic period, 300 years before Christ. Traditionally, the Jews felt that God alone was their teacher and that no human being should claim such a role.

Jesus recognized the tradition of disciples training to be teachers: "A disciple is not above his teacher... ; it is enough for the disciple to be like the teacher... " (Mt 10:24-25a) But he also reflects the older tradition of limiting the teacher role when he says, "But you are not to be called 'rabbi', for you have one Rabbi, and you are all brothers...Nor are you to be called 'teacher'; you have one Teacher, the Messiah." (Mt 23:8, 10, REB) The rabbinic era of Judaism, which continues today, pre-dates Jesus by producing such remarkable rabbi's as Rabbi Hillel, Rabbi Shammai, and Rabbi Gamaliel, all widely known prior to Jesus' ministry. The rabbinical structure and hierarchy was fluid during this time and only became formalized after Jesus' era.

In Jesus' day, a teacher could be called a rabbi without having passed through a required course of training. (John 7:15) Jesus was a charismatic teacher because he earned the authority and status of a rabbi in an untraditional way, through his own giftedness. He seized the authority of a rabbi rather than waiting for it to be granted. "By what authority are you doing these things? Who gave you this authority...?" (Mk 11:28)[29]

Jesus is frequently called rabbi or teacher throughout the four Gospels. According to the NRSV, it was the most common title in Mark and the second most common title in the Gospels of Matthew, Luke and John. We might presume, since this wasn't a title used in the churches to which these Gospels were written, that this truly hearkens back to Jesus'

Asian roots. Pauline churches, upon reading a Gospel for the first time, would likely not have recognized the title of teacher or rabbi for Jesus. They might also have been surprised that their title, "savior," is seldom mentioned (only three times) in the four Gospels. In those instances, it is likely a political claim defying Caesar as the mighty savior of the world. (Lk 1:69, 2:11; Jn 4:42) Of course, the four Gospels are not history books. They were written to influence and evangelize Europeans in the first century. But there is, nonetheless, a surprising reverence, particularly in the synoptic Gospels, for Jesus as a Palestinian, a Galilean, a rural peasant, an Asian teacher. The Middle Eastern context of his ministry is remarkably preserved given the fact that the intended audience was much more cosmopolitan, urban, sophisticated, pluralistic and western than the images of a farmer casting seed upon a path or a successful farmer building larger barns.

The Gospel of Thomas suggests an Asian approach in that Jesus is presented as a sage with his proverbs, parables and wisdom teachings. It is similar to the writings of many Buddhist and Asian teachers. "In classical Buddhist tradition the Buddha is a great teacher."[30] "Jesus and Lao Tzu were essentially teachers, enlightened sages, trying to convey their visions to humanity."[31] If you compare Jesus' wisdom teachings to that of the Buddha, they are strikingly similar. Marcus Borg says, "In their wisdom teaching, I see no significant difference."[32]

Japanese theologian Kosuke Koyama says, "Often I am reminded that Jesus Christ was present among the peoples of the world even before the arrival of missionaries,

Christians and churches. He goes ahead of us. He does not follow us. He says, 'Follow me!'"[33] Koyama reminds us of Jesus' teaching in Matthew 25 that whenever anyone feeds the hungry or clothes the naked they are doing it to Christ who is embodied though unrecognized among the poor. Koyama asks, "Is feeding the hungry, clothing the naked, visiting prisoners in the name of the Buddha an act of no value in the light of the name of Jesus Christ? Impossible."[34]

Those of us in the western world have seen little reason to turn to Jesus as an Asian Teacher. It doesn't serve our purposes any more than it would have served Paul's. Even when we took the Gospel to Asia over the past 200 years, it arrived at their shores in a westernized version. Jesus arrived back in Asia dressed in western attire. Recently, while traveling in Myanmar, I saw no drawings or paintings of an Asian or Burmese Jesus in Christian churches. I only saw the Swedish Jesus, blue eyes, white-skinned, fair, with European features. Indeed, in the west today many people are drawn to a more Mediterranean-looking Jesus, darker, and much closer to his Asian roots. I saw no such representation in Myanmar, and several leaders with whom I spoke knew of no such attempts. One author has written, "Jesus himself came from Asia, but what is his Asiatic face?"[35]

Choan-Seng Song, an Asian theologian, has said that Christians "who are not endowed with German eyes should not be prevented from seeing Christ differently. They must train themselves to see Christ through Chinese eyes, Japanese eyes, African eyes, Latin American eyes."[36] "This is clear: Jesus Christ cannot and may not be bound to one specific context, Western or Eastern. Responses to him have come and will continue to come from a great many different contexts."[37]

The Christ that was brought from the west to Asia was in many ways a "colonial Christ" not an Asian Christ. Kosuke Koyama again says, "I do not think Christianity in Asia for the last 400 years has really listened to the people. It has ignored people…Christianity has been busy planning…this campaign or that crusade…Christianity has become a one-way-traffic-religion…Christ-like going is not one-way-traffic. It is intensely two-ways. And in this two-way traffic with his people, Jesus gave up his right of way!…The amazing thing is that it is only in this way of giving up himself that Christ came to us…The crusade concept is a product of Christianity, not of Christ. The word is not found in the Bible… I submit that a good hundred million American dollars, a hundred years of crusading, will not make Asia Christian. Christian faith does not and cannot be spread by crusading. It will spread without money, without bishops, without theologians,… if people see a crucified mind, not a crusading mind in Christians, a two-way traffic mind…"[38]

If we had presented to Asians a more Palestinian Christ, a more Jewish Jesus, a more Asian Sage, it might have been more appealing. Instead, we took a Pauline westernized Christ, and we tried to westernize Asians instead of offering them the Asian Christ.

Yale Divinity School professor Lamin Sanneh suggests that because Paul immediately took Christianity from its Asian roots to a European audience, Christianity became a translated religion. "The fact of Christianity being a translated, and translating religion places God at the center of the universe of cultures, implying free coequality among cultures and a necessary relativizing of languages vis-à-vis the truth of God. No culture is so advanced and superior that it can claim exclusive access or advantage to the truth of God, and none so marginal or inferior that it can be excluded."[39]

Bernard Lee speaks of Paul's immediate translation of the gospel: "It is my conviction that profound contrasts exist between the world of Galilean Jews in Jesus' time and the Greek world that became the nurturing matrix for the emergence of a Christian church and a profound tradition of Christian doctrine…(I want to explore) the less traveled road of Galilean Jewish interpretation (that) was closed off for further travel…I would wish that early Syrian and Armenian communities had been retained as fuller spokespersons in the creation of Christian self-understanding. We might have had a Spirit christology as compelling as our Logos christology, and concomitantly, a humanity of Jesus as accessible as the divinity of Jesus. In fact, I wish that I knew more right now about the life of those early eastern Christian communities as well as about some of their contemporary expressions."[40]

In reality, we know something of the Asian Jesus, not just from the Gospels but from the early spread of Christianity eastward. It is far less known, but known nonetheless. Here are some examples:

"The Acts of Thomas," an early apocryphal writing, begins with Thomas being compelled to go to India: "At that time we apostles were all in Jerusalem…and we portioned out the regions of the world, in order that each one of us might go into the region that fell to him by lot and to the nation to which the Lord had sent him. By lot India fell to Judas Thomas, also called Didymus. And he did not wish to go, saying that he was not able to travel on account of the weakness of his body. He said, 'How can I, being a Hebrew, go among the Indians to proclaim the truth?' And while he was considering this and speaking, the Savior appeared to him during the night and said to him, 'Fear not, Thomas, go away to India and preach the word there, for my grace is with you.'" [41]

One tradition has it that Thomas came to India in 52 AD and landed on the Malabar coast. Coming to India was not difficult in the first century because of extensive trading routes. Numerous golden coins of the Roman Empire have been found all over the southern coasts of India. Diplomatic relations existed between India and the Roman Empire, and there were Jewish colonies in Malabar in the first century. St. Jerome in the 4th Century wrote about one leader sent by Bishop Demetrius of Alexandria, Egypt to "preach Christ to the Brahmins and to the philosophers of India" in AD 190.

Today, Thomas Christians in India trace their spiritual ancestry to St. Thomas. Their early practices were called Hindu in culture, Christian in religion and Oriental in worship. It was called during this early time, "The Thomas Way," originally a Buddhist term as in "Buddhism as a way of life."

Another example is the Nestorian faith that broke off from western Christianity in 428 AD and spread eastward from Rome. Through Syria and Persia, the Nestorian faith reached China between the 5th and 6th century. In 1623, a Nestorian Monument was uncovered that was carved in 781 AD, with an inscription praising God for this Christian movement in China.[42] This is also called The Church of the East.

The first state to embrace Christianity is purported to be Armenia in 301 AD and the Armenian Christians have maintained a continuous and rich history. The Assyrians claim to have the oldest church in the world at Edessa, founded soon after Jesus' death. The Jacobite or Syrian Orthodox Church traces it roots to the earliest Christian church in Antioch at the time of the apostles. The Eastern Orthodox Church has until recent times been a dark secret to the western church. The elevated role that Jesus plays in Islam and the Koran is yet another example of the Asian face of Jesus.

The Christian Church in Europe and America has spoken often of taking Jesus east. But *taking* Jesus east is a far different matter than *following* Jesus east.

On a recent trip to Myanmar, I read a biography of Adoniram Judson's life.[43] Throughout Myanmar, they call him "Dr. Judson," and even though a Baptist missionary in the early 1800's in a predominantly Buddhist nation, he is still revered. His Burmese-English Dictionary and his translation of the Burmese Bible are considered literary masterpieces even by Buddhists. The first thing the Judson's did upon arrival was to learn the Burmese language with a Hindu scholar serving as their teacher.

Judson began his ministry in Burma by building a zayat along Pagoda Road leading to the Shwe Dagon, the impressive Buddhist pagoda that sits atop the capitol city of Yangon. My hotel room in Yangon looked out upon the golden dome of the Shwe Dagon, and it brought great comfort to me each night as it reverently lit up the sky. Zayats were places for travelers to stop and rest, meet for conversation, and for teachers to teach their students. Judson's zayat was the site of the first Christian worship in Burma in 1819. Judson built a front porch to his zayat, and every day he would sit on the porch and call out to passers-by, "Ho! Everyone that thirsts for knowledge!" More people came until the teacher was fully occupied with his visitors.

By 1835, Judson spoke Burmese constantly. "He had now spent half his life in Asia, and could hardly 'put three sentences together' in spoken English. A visitor sent by the American mission board came to stay with the Judson's in March, 1836, and was struck by just how Burmese Adoniram had become…What struck the visitor the most was the worship of the local church of Moulmein. The congregation sat cross-legged on rows of mats. When Adoniram knelt in prayer, the Burmese would lean forward from the bamboo poles which served as back-rests, and rest their elbows on the floor. As he prayed, they would press the palms of their hands together in concentration. The only imported word in the service was the 'Amen' which everyone spoke aloud in response. At the end of the free time of prayer, Adoniram returned to his chair facing the worshippers, from where he could see everyone in the zayat."[44]

If only the missionaries who followed Judson would have become as Burmese, the shape and texture of the church there would be quite different today. If only they had followed Jesus eastward instead of taking Jesus eastward. By following Jesus eastward, the role of Jesus as Teacher would fit contextually into the role of teacher found in Eastern religions. And his agricultural stories certainly communicate well in the rural villages and hillsides of Asia. By following Jesus eastward, we might have sooner discovered the wisdom and sage tradition that many Asian religions hold in common, Christianity included. By following Jesus eastward, it might be easier to reconsider him as a teacher of shalom, a peaceteacher.

Shalom is actually an Asian concept, as it isn't dualistic, either-or, but a more holistic, inclusive idea. I was in dialogue one afternoon with a respected Buddhist teacher in Myanmar, and I was asking him what he and his community were doing to address the poverty, violence and injustice that surrounded their hillside community. I recall being disappointed in his answer as he spoke of the need for peace within. He told me that only as we meditate and discover peace within will the society around us know peace. I was listening to him with a western activist mentality. Shalom sees no break or separation between internal and external peace. Shalom within can create shalom beyond and between. His eastern understanding was closer to the idea of shalom than my own. Thich Nhat Hanh, the highly respected Vietnamese Buddhist wrote, "To work for peace, you must have a peaceful heart. When you do, you are a child of God. But many who work for peace are not at peace."[45] Jesus begins with this eastern understanding as he calls us to "receive shalom." This is a very different calling than one to "work for shalom." Often in my life I have wanted to change the world but not myself. However, Jesus also talks of "seeking shalom" by the intentionality of our actions, choices and lifestyles. His emphasis on spirituality and intentionality brings two worlds together.

Thich Nhat Hanh also said, "In Buddhism, practicing the teaching of the Buddha is the highest form of prayer. The

Buddha said, 'If someone is standing on one shore and wants to go to the other shore, he has to either use a boat or swim across. He cannot just pray, "Oh, other shore, please come over here for me to step across!"' To a Buddhist, praying without practicing is not real prayer."[46]

For the follower of Jesus, receiving shalom is the first step, but only the first. One must also seek shalom by working for justice, protecting the environment, reconciling with one's enemy, embracing community, practicing nonviolence. Shalom within cannot be kept within. Shalom within is drawn outward toward the seeds of shalom in the world. God is already introducing justice, harmony, nonviolence and reconciliation in the world. The Shalom of God is active between and among us, if we but have eyes to see it. (Mk 8:17-21) We seek shalom not by inventing justice but by joining God's Justice. We seek shalom not by introducing harmony or initiating peace but by joining the shalom within us with the shalom around us.

"The LORD bless you and keep you;

the LORD make his face to shine upon you,
and be gracious to you;

the LORD lift up his countenance upon you
and give you shalom."

Numbers 6:24-26

Endnotes

[1] p. 27, Willard M. Swartley, *Covenant of Peace*, Eerdmans Publishing Co., 2006

[2] p. 3, Robert James, *What is this thing called Aloha?*, Island Heritage, 2002

[3] p. 780, Vol. 2, *The New International Dictionary of New Testament Theology*, Zondervan

[4] p. 208, William Klassen, *The Anchor Bible Dictionary*, Vol. 5, Doubleday, 1992

[5] p. 22-23, Henri Nouwen, *Peacework*, Orbis, 2005

[6] p. 137-139, Marcus Borg, *Jesus, a New Vision*, 1987

[7] p.13, 15, ibid., Swartley

[8] p. 49, Vol. 4, The Anchor Bible Dictionary, Doubleday, 1992

[9] p. 15, ibid., Swartley, "The specific term 'kingdom of God' is virtually absent from the OT." P. 15

[10] p. 66, Marcus Borg, *The Heart of Christianity*, Harper San Francisco, 2003

[11] p. 23, ibid., Swartley

[12] p. 777, *The New Dictionary of New Testament Theology*, Vol. 2, Zondervan

[13] p. 76, p. 40, Walter Brueggemann, *Peace*, Chalice Press, 2001

[14] p. 120-121, Henri Nouwen, *Peacework*, Orbis, 2005

[15] p. 230, "Our God is Marching On!", A Testament of Hope, *The Essential Writings and Speeches of Martin Luther King, Jr.*, edited by James M. Washington, HarperCollins

[16] Metro-Goldwyn-Mayer Pictures, produced by Irwin Winkler and Rob Cowan, 1998; from a book by Oliver

Sacks, M.D.

[17]p. 299, April 16, 1963, *A Testament of Hope, The Essential Writings and Speeches of Martin Luther King, Jr.*, HarperCollins, edited by James M. Washington

[18]p. 64, John Dominic Crossan, Who Killed Jesus?, Harper Collins, 1995

[19] ibid., Crossan, p. 64

[20]p. 24, James H. Charlesworth, Hillel and Jesus, "Why Comparisons are Important," Minneapolis, Fortress Press, 1997

[21]p. 2, Parker Palmer, *The Courage to Teach*, San Francisco, Jossey-Bass, 1998

[22]ibid., Palmer, p. 11

[23]p. 182, Walter Brueggemann, *Peace*, Chalice Press, 2001

[24]p. 19, Walter Wink, *The Human Being*, Fortress Press, 2002; Wink translates "Son of Man" as "son of the man"

[25]ibid., Wink, p. xi

[26]p. 48, Colleen Ryan, Beyers Naude, *Pilgrimage of Faith*, David Philip, Cape Town, Wm. B. Eerdmans, Grand Rapids, Africa World Press, Trenton, NJ, 1990

[27]ibid, Ryan, p. 205

[28]p. 18, Bernard J. Lee, *The Galilean Jewishness of Jesus*, Paulist Press, 1988

[29]For further discussion of Jesus as charismatic teacher, see chapter 2 of my book, *Rabbi Jesus*, Smith & Helwys/Peake Road,

[30]p. 42, Paul Clasper, *Eastern Paths and the Christian Way*, Orbis, 1980

[31]p. xx, Martin Aronson, *Jesus and Lao Tzu, the Parallel Sayings*, Seastone 2003

[32]p. xi, Marcus Borg, *Jesus and Buddha, The Parallel Sayings*, Seastone, 1997

[33]p. 72, Kosuke Koyama, *50 Meditations*, Orbis, 1979

[34]ibid, Koyama, p. 73

[35]p. 19, Anton Wessels, *Images of Jesus, How Jesus is Perceived and Portrayed in Non-European Cultures*, Eerdmans, 1990; two Asian Christian artists whom I especially like are Chinese artist, He Qi, Chinese Christian Literature Council, 138 Nathan Road, 4/F. A. Kowloon, Hong Kong; and Indian Lutheran artist, Solomon Raj, asianchristianart.org

[36]p. 11, Choan-Seng Song, *Third-Eye Theology*, Orbis, 1979

[37]1ibid., p. 192, Wessels

[38]pp. 51-54, Kosuke Koyama, *Three Mile an Hour God*, Orbis, 1979

[39]p. 105-106, Lamin Sanneh, *Whose Religion is Christianity? The Gospel Beyond the West*, Eerdmans, 2003

[40]ibid., p. 8-9, Bernard Lee

[41] "The Acts of Thomas", 1, translation by J.K. Elliott, Apocryphal New Testament, Oxford, Clarendon Press

[42] internet sources: members.tripod.com/~Berchmans/early.html; www.yutopian.com/religion/history/Nestorian.html

[43]by John Waters, *Storming the Golden Kingdom*, STL Books, 1989

[44]ibid., Waters, p. 149

[45]p. 74, Thich Nhat Hanh, *Living Buddha, Living Christ*, Riverhead Books, 1995

[46]ibid., Thich Nhat Hanh, p. 79

Other Books by Stephen D. Jones:

Rabbi Jesus
Learning from the Master Teacher
ISBN 1-57312-099-5
Smyth and Helwys Publishing Co.
Peake Road, Macon Georgia
800/747-3016 • www.helwys.com

Faith Shaping
Youth and the Experience of Faith
Revised Edition
ISBN 0-8170-1118-8
Judson Press,
P.O. Box 851
Valley Forge, Pennsylvania 19482-0851
www.judsonpress.com • 800/458-3766

Stephen D. Jones is pastor of Seattle First Baptist Church. He has served churches in Michigan, Pennsylvania, Ohio and Colorado. He has been a life-long ecumenical and interfaith leader and peacemaker. The proceeds of this book benefit the Baptist Peace Fellowship of North America. Jones is a member of the board of the BPFNA.

ISBN 142511943-3

9 781425 119430